The Richest CAVEMAN

The

DOUG BATCHELOR

Story

As told to
Marilyn Tooker

A
**MOUNTAIN
MINISTRY
PUBLICATION**

Edited by Marvin Moore
Illustration by Lars Justinen
Cover Design by Penny Hall

Copyright © 1991 by

 **MOUNTAIN
MINISTRY**

5431 Auburn Blvd., Suite A-1 • Sacramento, CA 95841

All Rights Reserved
Printed in the United States of America
Remnant Publications, Coldwater, Michigan

This edition printed in 2005

Library of Congress Catalog Card Number: 89-62156

ISBN 0-8163-0876-4

91 92 93 94 • 5 4 3 2

Contents

1. Out With a Bang! 5

2. Military School 10

3. Runaway 16

4. Free at Last! 25

5. The Secret Cave 31

6. Crime Doesn't Pay 38

7. Shipped Out! 42

8. On the Road 49

9. The Arabs Are Coming! 52

10. New Mexico and Back 60

11. Discovering the Truth 70

12. Star for a Day 77

13. Trying the Churches 82

14. If at First You Don't Succeed 91

15. But Lord, I Could Never Be a Preacher! 99

16. Indian Tales 102

17. Going Home 111

18. The Rock That Would Not Roll 122

1

Out With a Bang!

I sat on the edge of my bed in my mother's New York apartment
and buried my face in my hands. Tears ran down my cheeks
and seeped through my fingers. I seldom cried, but this time,
something really broke loose. I had been in fights almost since
the day school started, and here I was in trouble again! I wondered if I would ever amount to anything. I just couldn't seem to
control my temper.

If Mom were here, maybe we could talk things over, but
that night she was gone. Since the divorce, she worked full time
and had less time than she would have liked for my brother
and me. Evenings, she either went out with friends, or sometimes had a party at our apartment. We seldom had an evening
at home together. But now Falcon, my brother, best friend, and
worst enemy, had gone to live with Dad in Florida. With his cystic
fibrosis, Falcon needed a milder climate, so here I was in the
apartment, alone, and desperately in need of someone to love me
and care what happened to me.

I thought of my beautiful mother. She had lots of friends,
most of them actors, writers, and singers. Her talent and good
looks made her the queen of every party. She was drawn to show
business like a moth to a flame. Her career really took off when
she started writing songs for Elvis Presley, but she had been
involved in show biz in one capacity or another ever since I could
remember. She wrote musicals for TV and plays, did bit parts in
movies, and worked as a film critic.

She used to take Falcon and me to work with her during
summer vacation, and we enjoyed all the attention from the stars.

5

They would come over and talk to us and tell us jokes between tapings. Some of the well-known ones that I still remember were Red Buttons, Frankie Avalon, Nancy Sinatra, Rowan and Martin, Maureen O'Hara, and Lloyd Bridges, but our favorites had to be the Three Stooges. How they made us laugh!

Yet something about the exciting people who made up the world of theater bothered me. As I got old enough to understand, I noticed that a frightening percentage of them were homosexuals, and it seemed that many of them were on drugs or alcohol, or both, yet they weren't happy. "Why do they work so hard to achieve fame when it makes them so miserable?" I wondered.

If Mom ever noticed the discrepancy in their lives, she never mentioned it. For her, the more excitement, the better. She used to have parties at our apartment, but all the guests wanted to do was sit around and talk and smoke pot. They would do dumb things like pop the bones in each others backs and laugh at their own stupid jokes. Some of them were so out of touch with reality! They looked like ghosts as they floated in and out of their own world. They seemed weird and lonely.

Lonely. How I hated the word! Sitting by myself on the edge of the bed, the events of the day crowded back into my mind, and as I relived the fight I'd been in, the scorching lecture from the principal, and my teacher's disapproving scowl, I felt lower than a clam. Who was I? Where did I come from? Why was I here? Those were not new questions. I often stared in the mirror and wondered. I'd been told that I was just another step in the process of evolution—an overly developed monkey. If that's all there was to life, why not get it over with?

I wasn't afraid to die. When you died, you just rotted and turned back into fertilizer—or so our teachers told us. I decided to swallow a bottle of sleeping pills, lie down on my bed, and' never wake up. Simple.

Resolutely, I stood up, wiped the tears off my hands onto my pants, and strode into the bathroom. Opening the door of the medicine cabinet, I stared at all the bottles and jars lined up neatly on the shelves. Which one had the sleeping pills in it? I knew Mom took one or two every night to go to sleep, but I hadn't paid that much attention to which bottle she used. I began taking them down, one by one, and reading the labels, but none of them said "sleeping pills." Finally I found one that said "Take one at bedtime. Valium." I was thirteen years old, but I'd never heard that word. I put the bottle back and continued the search, but nothing else sounded right, so I returned to the Valium. I unscrewed the lid, poured the whole bottle into my hand, and reached for a glass of water. My hand paused midair. What if these weren't sleeping pills? What if they were some kind of pills for ladies? What if they just made me sick? I didn't want to get sick. I'd had enough pain and misery. I wanted to die!

I leaned over and reread the label on the bottle, but I found no new clues, so I stood there for a long moment, trying to decide what to do. Slowly I reached for the bottle and poured the pills back inside. I'd find a better way to kill myself another day.

Looking back, I wonder how I could have been so blind to the clues that told me Mom cared. She tried to express her love in her own way. She would write a musical play for our class and put me in a starring role. She worked very hard at it, too: casting, costumes—even conducting the rehearsals herself. It took her away from her work, which meant smaller paychecks.

We enjoyed a certain togetherness before Falcon left. Sometimes we would sit around in the living room together watching TV. Mom and I would smoke pot, but Falcon couldn't because of his cystic fibrosis, so she made him cookies, putting in a generous amount of marijuana or hashish. Hashish was harder to find because it came from Turkey, and she only got it when some of her friends brought it back from their travels, but she would use some of it for Falcon's cookies. I thought, "That shows she must care."

Mom's maiden name, Tarshis, betrayed her Jewish heritage. My grandparents used to say we were related to Saul of Tarsus, but I think they were joking. When we moved to New York, my mom found that half the people in show business were Jews. She was proud of her Jewish heritage, but she had no interest in religion.

When my report card came out a few weeks after the big fight, I opened it with fear and trembling. My eyes scanned the page. Sure enough, my grades were a disaster. Quickly I closed it and shoved it into my pocket. How could I show this to Mom?

At home that evening my heart was filled with dread. I

knew she would yell and be upset, and probably end up crying. Again my thoughts turned to suicide. Maybe I could jump off the roof of our apartment building. I wondered if the door to the roof had been left unlocked. I took the elevator to the top floor and walked down the hall to the stairs that led onto the roof. I tried the doorknob, and it turned easily. I opened it, went up the steps, and walked out onto the roof. I climbed out onto the ledge that ran around the edge of the building and looked down. Sixteen stories. The street noises floated up to my ears: cars honking, engines revving, and sirens wailing in the distance. The people on the streets were so far below they seemed like ants scurrying about, all in a hurry.

"Why do they run around like that?" I asked myself. "Where are they all going?" I knew many of them were hurrying about trying to make money.

I thought of my father. He was wealthy—a multimillionaire. He hadn't been born with a silver spoon in his mouth, either. His father died when he was only seven. The oldest of four sons, he did what he could to help support the family. He sold newspapers on street corners and did every odd job that came his way to help feed the hungry little mouths at home. When his younger brothers got a little older and began working and contributing to the family income, my father took off at the ripe old age of sixteen with just a few cents in his pocket. World War II found him in the air force, flying and soaking up as much information about airplanes as he could.

Following his discharge at the end of the war, he struck out on his own. He had a keen mind and a sharp business sense, and soon he was building his empire. Eventually he owned two airlines and had numerous aircraft companies. He loved flying and airplanes so much that when my brother was born he named him Falcon, after the Falcon fanjet. He named me Douglas, after the Douglas aircraft. I think I came out ahead!

Flying his own plane became my father's favorite form of recreation, along with racing cars, whenever he could find the time, which wasn't very often. When he moved to Florida after he and Mom separated, he lived on an island so exclusive that special license plates or passes were required to enter the place. When I went to visit, I was glad he had a maid and a butler.

Out With a Bang!

Often they were all I had by way of companionship. Dad came to breakfast with me each morning, but he generally held a newspaper between us. If I spoke, he sometimes lowered his paper and answered, but other times he would just grunt. I was too young to realize that his busy schedule left him no free time, and the few minutes he could catch in the morning with his newspaper was the only time he had to himself all day. Yes, he had a Lear jet, a Rolls-Royce, security guards, and his own yacht, but he didn't seem happy. He was a driven man, for he determined never to be poor again. His life was so intense that he often worked sixteen-hour days, six days a week.

He grew up a Baptist, but religion had been thrust upon him by well-meaning family and friends, and he wanted no part of it. When his first wife and baby son were killed in a plane crash, I think he lost what little faith he had and considered himself an agnostic.

A gust of wind brought my thoughts back to the present. With my toes poking out over the ledge, I leaned over the edge of the building, hoping the next gust of wind would blow me off so I wouldn't have to muster the courage to jump. As I stood there hesitating, I remembered reading a few days earlier in the newspaper about a man who fell eight stories. He lost an arm and suffered a broken back, but he did not die. What if I didn't die? What if I ended up a cripple in constant pain? I shuddered!

Something else restrained me. I had a chronic case of curiosity. If I died today, what would I be missing tomorrow? Maybe I'd better stay around.

The nice thing about suicide is you can always postpone it. A few years later I would point that out to Mom when she called and told me she was going to commit suicide. It saved her life.

I climbed back off the ledge and sat down to think. The words to a beer commercial popped into my mind: "You only go around once in life. Grab all the gusto you can." That idea appealed to me. I would grab all the fun and excitement I could find. When I'd had enough, I'd do something big. Why go out with a whimper, like taking sleeping pills or jumping off a building? Why not go out with a bang!

2

Military School

Whenever I got into enough trouble at school, Mom would try to bail me out by finding another school for me to attend. In nine years I attended fourteen schools. If only my parents had recognized this misbehavior as a cry for love and attention, how different life could have been! But each, driven by goals of his or her own choosing, had things to think about other than a kid. I seemed determined to get into trouble and realized that my life was out of control. The more schools I attended, the less I learned. I could see I needed discipline and structure for my life.

One day Mom's friend Millie dropped by for a visit. "I'm going upstate [New York] to visit my sons at the military academy tomorrow," she said. "Why don't you and the boys come along? I'd like a little company, and I think your boys would enjoy seeing the school, wouldn't you, boys?" She had directed the question to Falcon and me.

"Sure," we said reluctantly.

I could still remember attending Black Fox Military Academy in California. Just five years old, I had been the youngest cadet at the school. However, what I remembered was pleasant enough, so I decided that I might as well see this one.

"It's the best military school in the country," Millie boasted as we drove along. "People send their kids here from all over the world. It's called New York Military Academy, but actually it is like the elementary school of West Point."

In my wildest dreams, I had never imagined such a school. Spacious green lawns stretched up to colorful flowerbeds next to ivy-covered stone buildings. A huge football field complete with bleachers lay at one end of the grounds, and the school had the largest indoor swimming pool I had ever seen. Most intriguing of all was the huge gym. Boys wrestled on mats in one area; two teams played a lively game of basketball in another. I peeked in doors that opened off the main room and saw boys lifting weights, beating punching bags, playing table tennis, and participating in all kinds of wonderful sports that I had only heard about. All this seemed a far cry from the brick or brownstone buildings behind chain-link fences I had attended in Manhattan. Ours were asphalt or concrete paved, with never a blade of grass. I was impressed when I saw the cadets in their sharp, handsome uniforms drilling in perfect formation on the parade ground.

I may have been out of control, but I was no dummy. I knew that what I saw was the result of discipline, obedience, and structure. Something inside of me cried out for this kind of order in my life.

"Mom, I've got to go to that school!" I blurted out after we got home. "I'm in trouble all the time, and I'm not learning a thing. This is just what I need!"

"I don't know, Doug," Mom said. "It's expensive, and I'm not sure you would fit into such a strict program. You'd be taking orders all day long. That's a *military* school." I couldn't blame her for being skeptical. I hadn't made good at anything yet. Why would this be any different?

As we sat around the TV that night eating ice cream, Mom and I smoking pot, the happenings at the military academy crowded my thoughts, and I brought up the subject of school again. "Please, Mom," I begged, "ask Dad what he thinks. It might be my last chance to make good."

"Ask for me too," Falcon piped up during a commercial. "See if we can both go."

Suddenly Mom's face lighted up, and I knew she had an idea. "I know; let's ask the Ouija board!" Although she had no particular religious beliefs, she leaned toward the occult. Many of her friends in show business were into astrology, palm reading, and seances. Mom went to the closet and hauled down the Ouija board, and we warmed it up by asking some trivial questions. Then, with the three of us resting our fingertips lightly on the indicator, Mom asked, "Should Doug go to military school?" We watched with baited breath. Slowly, it moved up and pointed to the word yes. It didn't seem very supernatural to me, because I had given it a little nudge.

"Should Falcon go to military school?" she asked next. It circled around a little, then moved slowly to the word *no*. Then a surprising thing happened. It moved up to the alphabet across the top of the board and spelled out the word *guns*. We looked at each other.

"No guns!" we each said in turn. I knew no one had helped it that time, and I couldn't understand what I had just seen. It didn't bother Mom, though. She got on the phone that very night and talked to Dad. In the end he agreed to let me give it a try and sent the money to finance the new venture.

I moved into the dormitory just after the new year. Carefully I put my belongings away in drawers and hung my shirts and coats in the closet. "They'll be impressed when they see how neat I am," I said to myself.

I had no idea how mistaken I was. There was a place for everything, and everything must be in its place. There were regulations about where clothes were to be hung and in what order, and there were regulations as to where our books were to be kept. There were even regulations on how long, wide, and thick our underwear must be folded and in what drawer it was to be stored!

The new guys were recipients of ridicule at every turn. We were frequently stopped in the hall by anyone with stripes. We were required to stand at attention, pull our chins in so far they doubled up, and repeat this phrase: "A new guy is the scum of the earth, sir." With *sir* between each word, it went like this: "A sir, new sir, guy sir, is sir, the sir, scum sir, of sir, the sir, earth sir, sir." And all this had to be said with a straight face. If you did not say it perfectly, you had to do it again. This would happen frequently.

Our day began early. Reveille blasted over the public address system at 6:00 a.m., and we couldn't dawdle. Roll call took place on the parade grounds at 6:30, and showers had to be taken before that. In the winter, if you hadn't dried your hair thoroughly before hurrying out onto the parade ground, it might freeze on your head. If you were one second late, you were late and dealt with accordingly.

Next we hurried to clean our rooms. Sometimes, if a guy's room didn't pass inspection, the sheets were ripped off the bed, his room was torn apart, and he had to start over. The sheets had to be stretched so tight that a quarter would bounce off them. Yet having to do your room over was no excuse for being late. We marched to meals and marched back, usually at double time.

They never hesitated to use corporal punishment—but not from a corporal! It was administered by the teacher, usually a hard-boiled military officer. I well remember the first time a teacher ordered me to bend over my desk. He drew back his army field belt, complete with metal grommets, and walloped my posterior with all his strength. My desk and I went flying, crashing into two other desks. I let out a yelp, and the room exploded with laughter. I was only eleven years old, but the teacher kept saying, "You're a man now; you're a man." I soon learned you didn't cry, and you didn't call home and complain, or you'd be laughed right out of school.

They didn't always whip you with a belt. Sometimes they just jerked you around by the hair or whacked you on the head. Even though all these boys were from wealthy homes, the officers pampered no one. My friend Rafael Trujillo, son of the dictator of the Dominican Republic, was just another guy at school. Rafael and I were good buddies and were together when he received word that his father had been killed in an accident in Spain.

They hassled me about the required church attendance on Sundays. "You must choose a church and attend every Sunday," they said. This was for their attendance record, of course.

"I can't," I told them. "If I attend only Jewish services, my dad will be mad. If I attend only Protestant services, my mother will be mad." They didn't like it, but there wasn't much they could do about it. I alternated between the Jewish and Protestant services. One Sunday I attended a Catholic church, but it bothered me that the priest smoked cigarettes while conducting the service, so I never went there again.

The picture of God that I had was not very pretty. In the Catholic and Protestant services, they told us, in essence, that if you were good, you'd go to heaven, but if you're bad, watch out!

God had a torture chamber called hell where you would roll and blister in molten sulphur and brimstone for all eternity. It didn't seem fair to me that God would punish the creatures He created for ever and ever just for the sins of one short lifetime. It also didn't make sense that God would throw somebody in hell before judgment day. I thought God was cruel, and I couldn't see how anyone could love Him. Later in life I was pleased to discover that this picture of hell was not biblical.

That summer Falcon and I went to camp on an island in the Caribbean where we snorkeled, water-skied, and did all the other things kids do at summer camp. I was bitten by a poisonous spider and almost lost my leg from the infection, and then tried to steal a sailboat and run away to a deserted island. Otherwise, it was a normal summer. Even though I enjoyed my freedom, I chomped at the bit, ready to take on another year at the military academy.

The second year hardly resembled the first year in any way, though. I soon found myself company clerk with the rank of sergeant. Each company had only one clerk, and my head swelled with pride as I looked at the new stripes on my uniform. Now I gave the orders instead of taking them—to other cadets, of course. I typed out reports, delivered papers, chased down medicines, and did any other errands that needed to be done. It was a job made to order for my free spirit. Now I had a legitimate excuse for being late and going wherever I wanted, whenever I wanted. Best of all, I felt good about myself, and I did my job well.

Coming from parents who were driven, I was naturally very competitive. Our room won inspection time after time, and I won medals in many sports, including wrestling, soccer, swimming, and diving. My grades took a sharp upward turn, and for the first time in my life I did well scholastically. I was more than a little pleased to be asked to teach others how to give shoes and belt buckles a spit shine. That year will always stand out in my mind as one of the happiest and most rewarding of my school days. I am sure I would have turned out to be an absolute slob had it not been for the training I received there.

But since we attended an all-boys school, we thought a great deal about girls. In fact, even the eight-and nine-year-olds talked of little else. I'm sure they weren't really as interested as they tried to pretend, but it was the macho thing to do, and they bragged with the best of us. I finally decided that girls were the most important thing for me, and there wasn't a single one on the whole campus.

Well, I didn't have to go to this school. Next year I'd go where there were girls!

3

Runaway

After a pleasant summer of snorkeling, water-skiing, and chasing girls, I returned to New York. Mom had found a private school called Bentley with mostly Jewish kids attending. The girls associated anyone from the military with glamour, and here I was, a prime specimen, physically fit, tanned, and confident. The boys respected me because I could fight, but my new-found acceptance proved to be my undoing. So desperate was I for love and acceptance that I immediately fell into bad habits. First, I began to steal a cigarette every day from my mother's stash so I could hang around and smoke with the others before school. But I didn't stop there. I began taking two a day so I could smoke one on the way home, too, and before long I was stealing money so I could buy my own.

I would do anything my friends dared me to do. Once, in Miami, I even jumped off a bridge into the bay. The crazier I acted, the more attention I got, and the kids began calling me "wild man." My grades grew progressively worse, until I found myself out of control and very unhappy.

One day after school a gang of us were hanging around the bus stop after school, smoking and talking. Two of the girls were really cute, and I wanted to make an impression, so on an impulse I said, "This school is a real drag. Nothing exciting ever happens around here. I think I'll run away."

A cute little blonde named Lou gasped. "Oh, no, Doug! You can't do that. Where would you go?" she asked, her eyes wide with concern.

"What would you do for money?" asked a good-looking brunette with creamy complexion.

"Aw, he won't go. He's just making noise," Rod challenged. Something of a bully, Rod didn't like all the attention I was getting. Before I knew it, I had backed myself into a corner, and the only way out was to go through with it or be laughed at. And that, of course, was unthinkable.

I lay awake that night planning what to do. I knew where Mom hid her cash, so I took $300 and caught a bus north toward my old stomping grounds. I hiked up into the hills near the military academy and camped for a few days. I could see the buildings from my camp, and I longed to be back. Every day in the woods I grew lonelier, until at last I gave up and returned home. At least no one could laugh at me now. Looking back, I wonder how I could have grieved my parents like that, but at the time I didn't think anyone cared about me, so I didn't care about anyone else either.

My first runaway experience spawned an idea for real adventure, and soon I began formulating a new plan. With a couple of friends I would go to Mexico, where we could do as we pleased and support ourselves by growing pot. I had one friend I liked, in particular. David McLean, a guy from India, had a winsome disposition and good looks and a flashy smile that attracted girls like honey attracts bees. It made me feel popular to be with him. He liked me for my crazy, daring ways, so we hit it off well. We would need a third person to help us, but who?

"Let's ask Victor," David suggested. "I've heard him talk about running away."

"I don't know," I said. "He seems like a nerd to me." But looking over the few possibilities, we finally decided to ask Victor and see if he'd be interested. He jumped at the idea.

"Bring your passports," I told them. "We don't want any trouble with the Mexican government."

"Where will we get the seeds to grow the pot?" Victor wanted to know.

"No problem," I assured him. "I know a friend who will sell me enough seed to start a farm. The problem will be how to get it into the country without being caught." We discussed several ideas, but finally hit on one we felt would be the perfect solution.

We cut a hole in the pages of a Bible and stashed the seeds there. At first it seemed sacrilegious, but since they raised no objections, I stifled my conscience.

We laid our plans carefully, and at last the day of departure arrived. "We'll meet at the train station," I told them. "Wear good clothes and dress neatly. They'll spot us in a minute if we dress like runaways."

But Victor wouldn't listen. When we met at the station he wore an old army coat, a dirty mechanic's cap, and tattered blue jeans. He had his possessions in a bundle on his back. He might as well have carried a big sign: "I am a runaway!"

We bought our tickets and lined up for the train. While we were waiting, three policemen came our way. I held my breath, but they walked right past David and me and surrounded Victor. They began asking questions. David and I acted as though we didn't know him and boarded with the other passengers. We found a seat together and sat down.

"Wow! That was a close call. You got it right about how to dress. They didn't even look at us!" David said excitedly under his breath. For a couple of hours we rode, talking under our breath, but our freedom was short-lived. In a small Pennsylvania town, several police detectives swarmed aboard the train and came slowly down the aisle of our coach.

"They're looking for us!" I whispered to David. "Let's go out the back." But other officers were waiting for us there. They had no trouble picking us out. Victor had squealed on us, told the police our names, what our plans were, and what we looked like. We soon found ourselves incarcerated with a ten-year-old boy who had killed an old woman with a baseball bat for her money. Just looking at him made my flesh crawl.

The man at juvenile hall treated us with great kindness, but I'm afraid I didn't appreciate his efforts. Being a Christian, he tried to tell us about God and His love, but I was so filled with prejudice from things my Jewish friends had said against Christianity that I didn't want to hear what he was saying.

We had been in juvenile hall for two days when we heard a key in the lock. The door swung open, and there stood two well-dressed detectives. "Get your things, boys. You're flying home.

Your mothers and some officers will meet you at the airport in New York, so don't try any funny stuff."

The knot in my stomach relaxed, and relief flooded my mind. I didn't relish facing Mom with the detectives, but maybe something would turn up.

As we boarded the plane, they returned our money and our personal effects. Wow! What a dumb move! That was all we needed!

At the airport in New York, attendants wheeled a set of stairs up to our plane, the hostess unlocked the door and opened it, and we could see people waiting inside. Dave and I filed out with all the other passengers, but instead of going into the terminal, we jumped some barricades and ran.

We expected to hear a police whistle or some kind of disturbance, but no one seemed to notice us. We hailed a cab and rode a few miles north. We watched the meter ticking away and glanced at each other with worried looks.

"Let us off at the train station," I told the cabby. "We don't want to use all our money for cab fare," I said under my breath to David. "The train doesn't cost much."

"Fine," he said, "but where shall we go?"

"They'll think we went south again," I said. "Let's go north. How about Haverstraw? I hear that's a nice little town. We can buy some camping gear there and go on up into the mountains."

"I'm with ya," David agreed. We purchased our tickets and boarded the train.

In Haverstraw we pooled our money and bought a tent and one sleeping bag. It got dark early, and as we hiked through a cemetery I could feel my heart throbbing in my ears. The back of my neck tingled as the hair stood up.

There were many strange contradictions in what I had been taught growing up. On the one hand, I was told that there is no God, that everything is just a big biological burp, with no life after death. But on the other hand, the same people told me there was a mystical side to life—a whole spirit world. Sometimes in our home we would have séances to communicate with the dead. This, plus all the horror films I had seen while growing up, didn't help the situation. I was sure we would never survive walking through a graveyard at night, especially in a full moon. I kept expecting some werewolf or vampire to jump out of the ground and do us in.

I hadn't read Ecclesiastes 9:5 in the Bible, which says, "The living know that they shall die: but the dead know not any thing"—or verse 10, which says there is no knowledge in the grave. I also didn't know that Jesus said the dead will sleep until the resurrection at the end of the world. I heaved a sigh of relief as we put a safe distance between us and all those tombstones.

As the moon rose higher, we pushed on and found a trail that led up into the mountain. The higher we went, the deeper the snow got, but being city boys, we didn't realize that the snow would be deeper and it would be colder at the top. Eventually we came to a small clearing among the trees, and I dropped the tent. "This looks good to me," I puffed.

"Yeah!" David agreed. "No one will find us here, and I'm wiped out and cold."

We set about erecting the tent. The moon shining on the white snow gave us quite a bit of light, and we soon had the tent set up. With a shelter over our heads, our thoughts turned to our empty stomachs. Though our fingers were stiff with cold, we slowly managed to open a can of beans and heat it over a can of Sterno.

"I'm gonna leave the Sterno burning," David said after we finished eating. "Maybe it'll warm the tent a little." We both struggled into our one sleeping bag fully clothed. Gradually we grew warm, and, though feeling very uncomfortable, we finally fell into an exhausted sleep.

We had gone to bed early, but we woke up a couple of hours later in a puddle of freezing water. The heat from the flame combined with our warm bodies had melted the snow under the tent, and we were soaked to the skin. We crawled stiffly out of the sleeping bag and stood looking at each other. Our teeth chattered, and our wet clothes stuck to our bodies.

"I don't know about you," I told David, "but I'm getting out of here."

"I'm with you," he said, "but what are we going to do with the tent and sleeping bag?"

"Leave 'em," I said. "The sleeping bag is wet and heavy, and I'm too cold to take down the tent. Let's get going."

We stumbled along down the mountain trail, which had a couple of inches of freshly fallen snow. I couldn't remember ever being more cold and miserable. We finally reached town, and the only thing still open was a small bar and restaurant. We gazed longingly at the warm glow within.

"Let's go in and get warm," I said. We entered and stood looking around. We saw a pool table at the back of the room and a couple of customers sitting on barstools eating hamburgers and French fries. They stopped and looked in our direction. I'm sure we looked like something the cat had dragged in, but we were too cold and hungry to care.

We climbed up on the stools and placed our orders. I had less than ten dollars in my pocket, but that was enough for a meal with a little to spare. I ordered a hamburger and a double order of fries. I wolfed down the burger almost without chewing it. By the time I started the French fries I had stopped shivering, and I felt even better after lighting a couple of cigarettes. We began talking to each other in low tones.

"This place is nice and warm," I told David. "Let's stay here. I don't want to go out in that cold again."

"But how?" he asked. "They'll soon be closing, and then we'll have to go."

"Let's play pool," I suggested. "Do you have any money left?"

"A little," he said.

"Good," I said. "Let's play as long as our money lasts. We'll think of something."

We played pool and smoked cigarettes until closing time. By then our clothes had dried out, and the world looked brighter. The owner approached us. "Time to close, fellows. You'll have to leave," he said, almost apologetically. We looked at each other helplessly.

"We can't," David blurted out. "I mean, we don't have any place to go."

"Yeah. We're looking for a job," I lied. "We got laid off work in New York, and we don't have money for a hotel."

The owner didn't seem to know what to say. After a long

pause, he said, "Hang on a minute." He left and went into the kitchen, where his wife busied herself with closing things down. Soon, he returned.

"Would you like to stay with us a few days? We can put you up and give you a little work. Maybe by then you can find something." We gratefully accepted his offer, glad for the promise of warm, dry beds and food.

But our new home lasted only a few days. They figured out the truth and reported us to the authorities as runaways. The police picked us up and took us to the station, and it didn't do any good to try to fool them. They dealt with runaways every day. They soon knew who we were and contacted our parents. David's mother picked him up the next day, but a policeman escorted me back to the airport in New York, where Mom was waiting.

"Thanks, Officer," she said. I could see that she was really hurt and angry. "How could you do this to me, Doug?" she cried. "I've done everything that I know to do for you. I can't take this any longer. You're going to live with your father! I've already bought your ticket. Your plane leaves in an hour."

A strained silence hung between us as we waited for my plane. I felt sorry for her. She was wearing sunglasses, but I could see that her eyes were red and swollen. We said stiff goodbyes to each other, and I boarded the plane. Slumping into my seat and staring blindly out the window, I burned with anger at myself and the world. The one thing I didn't want to do was live with my father. He was too strict.

I arrived sullen and depressed, and soon felt like an outsider in my dad's home. I couldn't help being jealous of my stepmother Betti and her son. She really tried hard to be nice to me, but I didn't give her a chance. I felt so unloved and unwanted that I made life absolutely miserable for everybody. Betti finally issued an ultimatum to my dad: "Either he goes, or I go." No one seemed very surprised.

Dad moved me into a hotel that he owned, and every day he would send a car to pick me up. Under the new arrangement, I worked half a day for him at the airport hangars and attended school half a day. I felt like a slave with no say about my life, and I hated it!

Dad began to get phone calls from the principal about once a week, reporting that I had cut class or wasn't doing my work or was being disruptive. Then Dad would pick me up, take me out to dinner, and we would talk. I liked it when he talked to me. I felt that he really cared, but he had trouble verbalizing his feelings.

He was verbal about one thing, though. He told me that if I didn't shape up, my next stop would be reform school, and I knew he meant it. I tried cooperating for a little while, but finally I couldn't stand it another day. I ran off again.

But I was in trouble before a day went by. My friend Joe and I decided to go swimming in the ocean. Neither of us had bathing suits, but it was dark, so we went skinny-dipping. We swam and played in the breakers for about half an hour. Then I said, "I'm gett'n hungry. Let's grab our clothes and run to that old abandoned beach house over there. We can stay in there till we're dry."

We scrambled out, snatched up our clothes, and streaked to the old house. The door creaked as we pushed it open. We closed it behind us and walked through the house.

"The wind's really starting to blow," Joe said. "Listen to those old shutters bang."

"I noticed that," I said. "Let's look around and see if we can find anything to use for a towel. We need to get dressed before someone comes to see what's making all the racket." We started checking the rooms to see what we could find, when the front door opened and in walked two policemen!

I'm not proud to say I was arrested for indecent exposure. I could have died from embarrassment, but I put up a bold front. They took us to the police station and interrogated us, trying to find out who we were, but I carefully concealed my true identity. I knew they would release me to my father as soon as they found out who he was, and that was the last thing I wanted. So I told them my name was Adam Fisher and that I was from New York. They kept me in jail about a week.

I began to wonder if I had made a mistake. White boys in this jail were in the minority, and the blacks and Cubans were pretty hard on us, but I hung on. Every day, the officers would question me, until one day I unintentionally gave the name of a real school I had attended. Within hours they had figured out who I was and called my father.

I sighed as I climbed into his new Lincoln. He didn't say a word as we drove along, but I knew he was at his wits' end.

Mom, always ready to try something new, discussed my situation with Dad. "He needs a school where he can express himself," she argued. "I've found a school called Pinehinge. It's an experimental free school up in Maine. Their philosophy is that kids will learn the things that are important to them. You know Doug will never study things he isn't interested in. This school is made to order for him."

Although he favored a school with strict discipline, Dad allowed himself to be persuaded. After all, his ideas hadn't worked, either.

4

Free at Last!

Mom was excited about Pinehinge. "You'll love it, Doug! You can choose any class you wish, and there are no required subjects. You can study whenever and whatever you want to. It's called a 'free school.'"

It sounded great to me. In fact, it was even more "free" than either of us suspected. The teachers were laid-back hippies, and there were only three rules at the school, which everybody ignored: "No drugs, no sex, and no fighting."

The dormitories were coed, and the rooms, too, for those who wished. There were about forty students, ranging in age from eight to eighteen.

You didn't have to get up if you didn't want to, you didn't have to go to class if you didn't want to, and you didn't have to go to meals if you didn't want to. That last bit of freedom would eventually cause the closing of the school.

We had been told we could learn whatever we wanted to, and we did. We learned how to sniff glue and how to make beer and LSD. In class we smoked cigarettes if we wanted, either tobacco or pot. There I met a kid from Brooklyn named Jay who introduced me to some of the finer points of burglary.

Jay and I had some things in common. His mother was Jewish, like mine. His father had had Mafia connections, but had been killed. Although Jay was fifteen and had a brilliant mind, the only written word he recognized was the *STOP* on stop signs. Other than that, he could not read. He had a dreadful Brooklyn accent that even some New Yorkers found difficult to understand, and I think he was even wilder, crazier, and more suicidal than I. On winter nights he would take me out to the vacant summer cabins up in Maine and show me how to break in and where to store the loot.

Since we didn't have to go to class unless we wanted to, I attended very few classes. I just wasted my time with friends and chased the girls. I did participate in the P.E. program, especially the snow skiing. Most of us had season passes to Mt. Abrams, and the school transported us up to the ski resort three times a week. I got to be a good skier that year. My friend Jay and I used to smoke pot on our way up the chairlift, and then do crazy, dare-devil things on the way down the slope. We didn't worry about getting hurt or even getting killed. I would dare him to jump off a high place, and he'd do it! He would find a higher place and dare me to jump off. We frequently went out of control and crashed, but somehow, we never broke any bones or injured ourselves seriously.

One day I saw a notice on the school bulletin board:

SILVA MIND CONTROL
Learn how you can
win lotteries, heal people,
make things happen,
and control your life.

Now that sounded like a class worth taking! I decided to go.

The class lasted for about two weeks. The teacher would present a new concept, and we'd discuss it and ask questions. Then we'd break up into small groups and practice. "The subconscious is more powerful than the conscious," our teacher explained. By a type of self-hypnosis, we were taught to reach into the deeper levels of our mind. It was represented as working with God—something of which God approved—when it was actually the opposite. "Jesus," our teacher explained, "had discovered how to use the powers of the mind, and that's how He healed people. God is within you. You are god." Not knowing the Bible, we didn't realize that we were cooperating with Satan. We had never heard that sorcery was forbidden in Holy Scripture and that Satan transforms himself into an angel of light. I had never heard of Ephesians 6:12, so we simply believed what our teachers told us. A supernatural power attended our experiments, and we felt it.

Some students boasted of their newly acquired power. A group of us stood in the hall one day excitedly discussing the "experiments" we had done.

"I don't believe it!" Laura said scornfully. "You think something is happening, but it's really all in your head." Laura had not taken the class.

"But something does happen," I declared confidently. "There's power in this thing, and I can prove it."

"Oh, yeah! How are you going to do that?" Laura asked.

"I'll heal somebody," I said. "No, I'll *diagnose* and heal them. You just tell me who you want healed, and I'll do it!" I challenged.

"You're on!" she said, looking me squarely in the eye. "Name the time and place. I'll be there."

We decided to meet in the lounge at seven o'clock after dinner. I arranged a couple of chairs in a quiet corner while I waited.

"Sit down," I invited when she arrived. We sat facing each other. "What do you want me to do?" I asked.

"I want you to diagnose someone who is ill—tell me what's wrong with her."

"You'll have to give me her name and address," I said, and she did. It took only minutes for me to reach that state of self-hypnosis called the alpha brain level. A picture of a woman flashed onto my mental screen, and I began to describe her. "I see a woman, about forty-five years old. She's a brunette, wearing glasses. She is medium in build."

"Oh, no! I can't believe this. That's my mother!" Laura slapped her hand to her forehead.

Then I began a journey down through her mother's body to locate the problem. When I came to her reproductive organs, I could see something wrong. "Your mother is sterile," I announced. She can't have children."

Laura's mouth dropped open. "How did you know that? How could you tell? I've never told anybody, but I'm adopted because my mother can't have children! Can you help her?"

"I'll try," I said. I went deeper into my subconscious. We

27

had been warned not to go too deep, or we would lose control. I can't remember how I did it, but I performed some kind of psychic surgery. I never learned the results. If I had known then what I know now, I would have been frightened.

Evan Owens—a most unusual personality—and I became good friends. He was only thirteen, but he had an IQ of 165. His parents sent him to Pinehinge in hopes of finding something that would challenge his genius, but he took little interest in anything. He enjoyed drinking and smoking pot along with the rest of us. Some bright kids I had known were bores, but not Evan. He had a wit that kept us laughing. He even looked comical. His hair, which he wore in an Afro that stood out about a foot, contributed to his funny looks. It made his head look like a giant ball of dandelion fuzz. When he got up in the morning, he really looked strange, because his hair would be flat on the side he slept on.

"Let's go to town and get a couple of six-packs of beer," Evan proposed one day. "It's too quiet around here."

"Sounds good to me," I said. I had a driver's permit from Florida on which I had changed my date of birth from 1957 to 1952, which made me "legally" old enough to buy alcoholic beverages.

The staid little town of Waterford, Maine, with its respectable, churchgoing people, looked with disgust at the students of Pinehinge, and with good reason. The students not only looked like something out of a bad dream with their old clothes and long, greasy hair, they also insulted the residents with obscenities and bad language and were accused of teaching Communism and selling their children drugs.

As we made our purchase in the store, I noticed a man glaring at us. He was dressed in a camouflage suit and hunter's hat. I tried to shrug off the chill that gripped me, because I recognized that insane look of violence from my days on the streets of New York City. When he followed us out the door and climbed into his pickup, I knew he was up to no good. I glanced at his pickup and noticed a gun rack in the rear window that held a rifle and a shotgun. Evan noticed the guns too. When we were about a quarter of a mile down the road, the man started his motor and began to follow us slowly.

It wasn't hard to guess what he had in mind. He planned to follow us to the edge of town, and when we were far enough into the woods, he would do in a couple of hippies. No one would know the difference, and even if we were found, no one would care.

Evan and I took turns looking back and trying to act cool. Suddenly, Evan gasped. "Doug! He's stopped the truck and is going for his gun!"

"Let's beat it!" I said. We left the road and crashed into the woods, little noticing the briars that grabbed and scratched us or the limbs that slapped us in the face. With all that adrenaline pumping through our systems, our feet fairly flew. We soon out-distanced him, and when we felt we were far enough away, we dived into the brush. Our hearts pounded in our ears, and pain stabbed our chests as we forced ourselves to breathe quietly.

We heard him go tromping by not far away. Soon he stopped, and we knew he was waiting for us to come out. Then he began shooting into the bushes, trying to flush us out. The report from the gun was so loud that I remember leaves falling from the trees, just from the sound. A bullet zinged over our heads and slammed into a tree behind us, showering more leaves down on us. After a few minutes we heard his steps receding in the distance.

We lay on the ground for an eternity. I heard a paper bag rustle, and I looked at Evan, startled. He pulled a six-pack out of the bag as quietly as he could.

"What are you doing?" I asked incredulously. I thought with his creative genius he might be planning a diversion. Instead, he pulled a can of beer from its plastic collar and proceeded to pop the tab. The beer spewed high after the good shaking it got from our running. Evan put the can to his lips and drew a long swig.

"If I'm going to die, I want to be drunk," he whispered. By the time he had guzzled his second can, his inhibitions fell away. He stood to his feet and began to peek through the bushes.

"He's gone!" he whispered loudly. I got to my feet as quietly as possible, and we began tiptoeing toward the road, watching all sides, looking for a place to jump if we saw our assailant again.

About 150 yards down the road we saw him. "There he is, sitting in his pickup," I whispered in a panic. Apparently he decided to wait us out. He probably figured we'd eventually return to the road.

"I hear a car coming!" I told Evan breathlessly. We watched as it came into view. Our hearts skipped a beat as we saw Dottie, one of the teachers from Pinehinge, behind the wheel, driving some students back to school. We ran out of the woods and stood in the middle of the road waving and yelling, "Stop! Stop!" She had no choice but to stop or run us over. She rolled down her window.

"I can't take you back to school. My car is full," she said.

"You've got to!" I yelled. "Do you see the guy in that truck down the road? He's been shooting at us!" He had just started up his truck again. She took in the situation at a glance.

"Get in, quick!" she urged. We piled in on the other kids and slammed the door behind us. She peeled out, driving furiously toward the school. A little later, when she checked the rearview mirror, he was gone, and we began to breathe again!

Since some of us seldom got to meals, we had to find an alternative. At first we raided the kitchen and helped ourselves. Then one day we found a padlock on the door. No problem. We simply tunneled into the basement, where the food was stored, and helped ourselves. They kept changing the padlocks, but they never learned about the tunnel. We stole so much food that the school went bankrupt and finally had to close its doors.

Did all this "freedom" make me happy? Hardly. I'm sure that was one of the most miserable years in my life. I could see no purpose to life. I was happier in military school with all of its rules than at the free school with no law or regulations.

5

The Secret Cave

Colorful rumors reached our ears about the hippie communes and the great climate of southern California. It never got cold, even in winter. You could camp out and eat off the land. "That's the kind of life I want!" I told Jay. "I want to live off the land and not be accountable to anybody."

"Yeah, man!" he said enthusiastically. "We're fifteen years old. We can take care of ourselves. Let's go look it over!"

During spring vacation we took off from Pinehinge, hitchhiking to southern California. We camped on the outskirts of Palm Springs. One day some hippies gave us a ride into town in their old van. "Where's a good place to hang out?" I asked. "You know, a place to party."

"Tahquitz Canyon is where we go," the tall, bearded guy told us. "It's far enough from town so the cops don't bug us, and we can smoke our reefers, drink beer, and make all the noise we want. We're heading over this afternoon. Wanna come with us?"

I looked at Jay. "Far out!" we said in unison.

Although Tahquitz Canyon is fifteen miles long, most people went only to the mouth by Palm Springs to party and waste time. The beauty of the place took me by surprise. There were trees and grass tucked away in this remote desert valley, and the waterfall captivated me. It seemed to be a living creature as it cascaded over the great, smooth boulders. It took the long plunge to the rocks below, and then it rose up in a silvery cloud, and as the sunlight caught the droplets, it created a lovely rainbow. No wonder some of the movie directors used it as a backdrop for their films!

While we were all kicking back and smoking pot, a man

31

and a young woman walked down out of the canyon. His long hair had been bleached white by the sun, and his dark, leathery skin and shapeless beard reminded me of a mountain goat. His bare feet also intrigued me. How could he walk barefooted with so much cactus around? I wondered.

She followed along behind, a beautiful girl about eighteen years old, with large brown eyes, flowing dark hair, and smooth olive skin. She looked like a mixture of Hawaiian and Italian. In a backpack seat she carried a most curious-looking baby. His sun-darkened skin contrasted dramatically with his white hair that stood on end as though he had stuck his finger into an electric socket. I learned that he had been born in Tahquitz Canyon, and they named him Tewey Tahquitz.

"Where ya comin' from?" I asked the man. He paused and looked at me.

"From home," he answered.

"Ya mean you live up there?" I motioned toward the canyon. "Wa' d-ya live in?" I tried to imitate the hippie lingo.

"Oh, a cave," he said nonchalantly.

Now this city boy could hardly suppress his surprise. "Man! I'd sure like to see your place. Mind if I go back with ya?" I asked eagerly.

"Be my guest," he answered. "We're hiking into town t' panhandle, get some groceries, and try t' give away these coyote puppies while we're there." He held up two of the cutest pups I had ever seen.

"The mother is part dog, part coyote," he explained. "The father's all coyote. We'll probably be back in a couple a' hours. Ya can follow us up when we get back."

I waited impatiently for their return. Jay lay on the ground with eyes half open, too stoned to know what was going on. When they finally returned, I fell in behind them, and we started up the canyon.

"My name's Jim," he said as we walked single file up the winding trail, "and this's m' wife, Sunny."

I asked lots of questions as we walked, but soon the gentle grade gave way to a steeper, rockier path. I was breathing so hard I had to stop talking, though I did ask every little while, "How much farther?"

Jim would say, "Oh, not far. It's just around the hill."

I saw a small hill ahead and felt sure I could make it that far. I soon learned, however, that he was talking about the mountain up ahead. It didn't take me long to discover how soft I had become. After leaving military school I started smoking, and not just cigarettes. In fact, I had smoked pot that very day, which made climbing even harder, but they walked on, talking and laughing as though it were nothing. He carried a forty- or fifty-pound backpack of food, and she carried food and a baby. I had only myself and could hardly keep up.

The sun went down, and it grew darker and darker. I wondered how they could see where to go. I could only see the tops of Sunny's white socks above her boots. They seemed to jump up and down as she walked. I stumbled along uphill after her, sometimes on all fours, trying to keep up. Finally, I asked him, "Don't you want to stop and take a break?"

"Naw, this ain't the place where we usually rest," he said. Fortunately, I bumped into some cholla cactus a couple of times, and though it stung painfully, at least they stopped and waited for me to pick out the stickers, which gave me a chance to catch my breath.

"How much farther?" I asked.

"Oh, just a little farther."

In New York, "a little farther" meant a block or two. To him, however, it was more like a mile or two, and uphill at that. Finally we reached the top of the ridge about 4,000 feet above Palm Springs. What an incredible sight! We could look down on the dark desert and see the lights of Palm Springs, Desert Hot Springs, Cathedral City, Palm Desert, and Indio spread out below us. They smoked a little pot while we rested. I had just begun to catch my breath when they picked up their packs and set off again.

"Is it much farther?" I asked.

"Naw," he assured me. "From here on it's downhill most of the way." It was downhill, all right, but it was so steep that every step jerked my legs, and I had to dig in my heel to keep from sliding. Then I noticed the sound of water running, and soon we began zigzagging across a creek. They knew where the rocks were, but I kept slipping and getting myself wet, not to mention the tree branches that kept slapping me in the face. The desert floor had given way to a jungle up here where there was water.

Just when I thought I couldn't take another step, we reached the cave. Jim lit a candle, but I was too tired to look about. I just watched as Sunny unrolled a damp sleeping bag. "You can sleep here," she said. "We're going up to our summer cave."

"Summer cave?" I asked apprehensively. They disappeared into the dark and left me all alone in this eerie spot. I crawled into the damp sleeping bag and curled up into a tight ball. I could hear rustling noises that I later learned were mice, but in my mind they could have been slithering rattlesnakes or a mountain lion creeping up on me. I was too tired to care. I finally felt warm enough to drop off to sleep with the sound of the coyotes howling in the distance, mournful owls hooting into the night, and the rustling noises in the cave.

When I woke up the next morning, if I hadn't been so sore, I would have thought I had died and gone to heaven. The sun shone in all its splendor, a quiet pool of clear water fed by a small gurgling stream lay almost directly in front of the cave, and some birds warbled cheerily not far away. Jim and Sunny had returned and were sunbathing on a rock not far from me, wearing their birthday tuxedos. The baby played by the water, and nearby the mother coyote dog sprawled, nursing her remaining puppies. The smell of food cooking on the open fire reminded me that I hadn't eaten for a long time, and the aroma made my mouth water.

I hardly knew how to act in the presence of two naked people. I never did get completely used to it at that time, but after a while it seemed natural enough that I could pretend not to notice. I found their way of life much to my liking. They lived, to a great extent, off the land. There were wild grapes and berries, Sunny made a tasty dish from a certain part of the cattails, and they had a vegetable garden. They even grew their own pot. Wild bighorn sheep roamed the mountains. Though the sheep were protected by now, when they wanted meat, Jim would simply go out with his gun and bring home a sheep or a deer.

I knew I couldn't stay. I had left Jay in camp, and he would be expecting me, but I made up my mind that some day I would be a cave man.

The Secret Cave

The next day Jay and I hit the road again. We ended up in Santa Monica, very nearly broke. The sun edged toward the horizon as the driver pulled to a stop at a corner.

"I'll let you out here," he said. "I'm turning east."

"Thanks for the ride," we both said as we pulled out our packs and shut the door.

"Well, where we gonna spend the night?" Jay asked. "I wouldn't want to sleep on the streets here, not knowing anyone."

"Let's ask someone where we can get a cheap room," I suggested.

"Hey, man, I don't have much money left," Jay objected.

"Me neither, but maybe we can find something real cheap." Down at the corner, some street people sat smoking and talking. I approached them. "Is there anywhere around here a poor man can eat and crash for the night?"

One of them pointed down the street. "There's a flophouse a couple of blocks that a-way. You can stay there for three dollars a night."

"Yeah," another spoke up, "and there's a mission two blocks over where you can get a free meal. All you have t' do is listen to their preachin', and they feed you. Just be there at eight o'clock in the morning. That's when they close the doors and lock them. If you're not there on time, you'll get left out."

"Thanks," we said, and we started walking in the direction of the flophouse.

The woodwork looked grimy, and strips of wallpaper hung in places at the old hotel. We paid our three dollars and were given a set of semiclean sheets and a towel apiece.

"You can have room 218," the clerk at the desk said, handing us our key. "The bathroom is down the hall on your right." The place had an "old" smell about it—a combination of stale cigarette smoke, cheap wine, and urine. At least the sheets were supposed to be clean.

It wasn't easy to get up early the next morning, but along with twenty or twenty-five others, we gathered in front of the mission. The doors opened promptly at eight o'clock, and we all poured in. Jay and I sat near the back.

The group at the mission gave a nice program and treated

us with utmost courtesy and patience, regardless of how we behaved, which was awful. A smiling bald man stood up and gave his testimony, while the people around me were talking and making jokes. One slob burped loudly, and everyone laughed. But through it all the bald-headed man continued his testimony, radiating a smile of genuine happiness. Someone in the row in front of us threw up all over the floor, and one of the mission staff rushed over and cleaned it up, while another helped the poor fellow to the bathroom. After his testimony the bald man sang us a song. All this time people were passing out, some dead drunk, others from fatigue or hunger. God's angels must have beheld us with pity.

One of the young men who helped with the program had a compact, muscular body like Mr. Universe's. He could have taken two or three of the loud-mouthed troublemakers and bashed their heads together. Instead, he stood up and gave a ringing testimony of what Jesus Christ had done for him. At the end he invited us to give our hearts to Him too. I detected his sadness when nobody responded.

When the program ended, we were ushered into a back room, where tables were covered with white tablecloths and everything appeared clean. I must have been expecting bread and water, because I remember how it surprised me to be served such good food. We stood in line to receive our ration—a large bowl of homemade stew, a generous serving of bread, and a cup of coffee. They even gave us dessert—cherry pie!

I couldn't understand it at all. Here we were, dirty, uncouth, and rude, yet they treated us with dignity and respect, as though we were decent human beings. Somehow it didn't track with what I had been told about Christianity.

We heard about another place that served free meals—the Hare Krishna temple. One day we decided to try it. We had to attend their service too—two hours of it. Some people claimed that it was a counterfeit religion, and it did differ widely from any Christian service I ever attended. The men shave their heads, leaving only a little ponytail in back. Their saffron robes are loose and flowing. The women also wear loose, flowing robes in pinks, blues, and purples. While the bass guitar and drums play a monotonous beat, the people sway and jump in rhythm, shake their tambourines, wave their arms, and leap through the air. As they are doing this, everyone chants a monotonous chant: "Hare Krishna, Hare Krishna, Krishna, Krishna, Hare, Hare; Hare Ramah, Hare Ramah, Ramah, Ramah, Hare, Hare . . ."

I could see immediately that the people were being hypnotized. I had been around show business enough to recognize that. Hypnosis takes advantage of certain properties of the optical and auditory nerves. The thumping, thumping rhythm puts the person into a hypnotic state. When a nonsensical phrase is repeated over and over, the mind forms a subconscious thought. After a while the mind is so filled with these empty, vain thoughts that it blots out the real worries and frustrations of life, giving a false sense of peace—a kind of euphoria. This inner peace is supposed to be God. Under this spell people happily give away their property and money.

When I saw what was happening, I went into the bathroom and stayed throughout most of the service, especially during the chanting. When I came out I noticed that Jay seemed to be enjoying it, and I began to worry about him. After a meal of yogurt, which I'm afraid I didn't appreciate very much, I grabbed Jay, and we got out of there.

Spring vacation had been over for several days already, and here we were, clear across the country from our school.

"We'd better get back to school if we're going to," I said.

"What's the hurry?" Jay protested. "This is spring break, remember?"

"Yes, and I also remember the break ended two weeks ago, and it'll take us another week to get back. Come on. Let's go."

6

Crime Doesn't Pay

After school at Pinehinge, I returned to Florida to spend the summer with Dad, but it just didn't work out. Pinehinge had fed my thirst for unrestrained freedom, and my father found me completely unmanageable.

"Doug," he said to me one day, "I am at my wits' end. I don't know what to do with you. If you can't cooperate and live like a decent human being, you'll have to leave," and with a broken heart, he watched me storm off into the world. I had turned sixteen in March.

Hurt, bewildered, and angry, I set out, not knowing where to go. I reached the turnpike and headed north on Interstate 95. I joined up with a tall fellow named Scott. He had a muscular build, and the glasses he wore gave him an educated appearance, though he had scarcely been to high school.

Together we hitchhiked from Miami to Boston, where Scott had been living before he went to Vietnam. We soon found jobs and were doing fairly well, but before long I realized that Scott was supplementing his income with a burglary business. Gradually I found myself going along with him and, before I realized what was happening, I fell into a complete life of crime.

For the next few months, I reached a low that caused me to despise myself and all mankind. Scott and I lived in flophouses and stole cars, TVs, and anything we could that could be converted into cash.

Trying to live on your own in a big city like Boston has its drawbacks for someone who is only sixteen years old, but before long I was able to obtain a Massachusetts driver's license that said I was eighteen. With my false I.D. I found a part-time job as a security guard with a company called Business Intelligence. It came complete with a badge, uniform, and billy club. It made me feel important to put the badge in my wallet and flash it when buying alcohol. My new position also gave me inside information for burglary jobs.

While working as a security guard, I met a young man named Brad who was also a security guard. A rather quiet fellow, he was involved in an Eastern religion called Shakti. Brad knew about my stealing. "Doug," he said, "you're going to pay for what you're doing some day. You aren't really getting away with anything."

"What do you mean?" I asked.

"I mean, that's your karma. What goes around comes around. The things you're doing to other people will be done to you.

"That's crazy, man!" I cried. "I stole a TV; I got rid of it. I didn't get caught, and I never will."

"You'll see," he said simply.

A few days later someone broke into my apartment and stole my TV set and a radio, and boy, was I mad! Then I began to notice that whenever I stole something, it would be stolen from me. When I stole money, it would disappear! I learned later that Scott was stealing from me! I stole a car and promptly got two flat tires. What really convinced me was a small trifle, but the coincidence was so remarkable that it frightened me. While at someone's house, I stole an unopened box of Krusteaz whole-wheat pancake mix with the price $1.19 stamped on it. (I drank, smoked, and used drugs, but I insisted on eating whole wheat because that was healthful!) When I got home, I found that some of my friends had come by and helped themselves to my brand new jar of Tang and used it all. By the empty jar was the lid, with a price tag on it that said $1.19!

"This is spooky!" I said to myself. "Somebody out there sees me and knows what I'm doing!" For the first time in my life, I really believed in my heart that there was a God!

When Brad invited me to one of his meetings a few days later, I quickly agreed to go. As a matter of fact, I went to several in the coming weeks. I didn't understand most of what I heard, but I usually came home with more books and less money.

The Richest Caveman

As I sat reading the newspaper one evening, a piercing scream and footsteps pounding down the hall catapulted me to my feet. I opened the door a crack, and I could see Sugarman—a black pimp who lived on our floor—beating one of his girls. She broke loose from his grasp and ran. He hurled a broom after her, and I closed the door.

"I hope he doesn't kill her," I thought as I sank back into my chair. Fights and stabbings were commonplace in this run-down rooming house, but I couldn't get used to it. I flicked the ashes from my cigarette. "What am I doing living in this dump and sharing a bathroom with these creeps? I can't even sleep at night with all the partying and carrying on. I'm sick of this room, and I'm sick of this kind of life!"

The phone rang, and I picked it up.

"Hi, Doug. This is Dad!" said the voice at the other end of the line. "I've been up to New York on business and stopped off to say Hello." He sounded cheerful, and I was glad to hear his voice. "Would you like to get together for an hour or two?"

"Sure, Dad. Can I take you to dinner?" I asked. I wanted to be sure he knew that I had my own money.

"Well, I planned to take you to dinner, but why not? Just tell me where to meet."

I knew some fancy restaurants in Boston, and I wanted to impress him, so I named the most expensive one I could think of and gave him the address.

I arrived ahead of him and stood outside waiting. Soon a cab pulled up, and Dad climbed out. A feeling of gladness swept over me, and I longed to rush over and throw my arms around him, but hugging just wasn't done in our family. We just grinned at each other and shook hands.

In the restaurant, the waiter seated us, and we chatted a short while. After we had ordered, he came to the point of his visit. "Doug, I feel like I've failed you, and I'm sorry. Will you give me one more chance?"

Tears almost came to my eyes at this unexpected confession. I hesitated. "What do you want, Dad?" I asked cautiously.

"Well, it's about your education," he said. "You really should be in school. You're only sixteen, you know."

"But, Dad"—my temper began to rise—"I've been doing a

good job of taking care of myself!" I pulled a large roll of bills from my pocket and held it out for him to see. He wasn't impressed. "Anyhow, you know how I feel about school."

He raised a restraining hand. "Now wait a minute, Doug. Hear me out. I was talking to a friend of mine, and he told me about this school on board a ship. It's a sailing vessel, and it sails all over the world. The students are the crew. You have classes on board the ship, and they make stops in all sorts of exotic places. You can come and go as you please and do all kinds of things. You can scuba dive and water-ski, and there are plenty of girls. The school year has just started, and the ship is somewhere in the Mediterranean right now."

It sounded too good to be true. "What's the name of the school?" I asked, careful not to sound too interested.

"It's called The Flint School Abroad," he said.

"Well, I don't know." I hesitated. We sat in silence for a long time. I wasn't sure I would ever fit into a structured program again, where I'd have to take orders. Still, it sounded like fun, and frankly, I was tired of fending for myself. Finally I said, "Maybe I'll give it a try."

A look of relief passed over my father's face, and I could see tears in his eyes. Inwardly, I rejoiced. If only I had known what lay ahead!

7

Shipped Out!

Dad cancelled all his business appointments so he could fly with me to Genoa, Italy, where the school was docked. We truly enjoyed being together on that flight, and I knew he cared about me. He even patted me on the back as we walked together aboard the ship. After helping me register and carry my belongings aboard, he squeezed my hand as we shook, and said goodbye. "Good luck, son. Work hard, and I'll see you at Christmas."

"OK, Dad," I said. After he left I put my belongings away and went out to explore on my own.

It didn't take me long to size up the kids who comprised this school. Many were the sons of senators and politicians who, like me, were wild, without restraint, and a threat to their fathers' reputations back home. If they were out of the country, no one would hear about them. Others were delinquents, the sons of wealthy parents who couldn't be bothered with all the problems of youth. They simply turned their parenting responsibility over to the school. Several of the boys accosted me during my first few days. "Did you bring any drugs?"

What Dad had been told about this school turned out to be only *partly* true. Actually, we were prisoners, in a sense. We could not fraternize with girls, and naturally we were not allowed to drink, smoke, or use drugs. They took away our passports when we went ashore. In a country like Italy, they would lock you up and throw away the key if they caught you without a passport, so we didn't dare do anything that would attract attention. I never did any scuba diving, water-skiing, or sports the whole time I was there.

The school's science program centered around the evolutionary theory, and those who believed in creation were ridiculed as idiots. The films shown in class portrayed Darwin as a hero.

"There is no God," the teacher told us. "You have to make it on your own. If you have to step on somebody to reach your goal, do it. If you don't, somebody else will." This cold philosophy left me feeling more lonely and isolated than ever.

I was still searching for God through Eastern religions like Shokti, and I didn't want anybody telling me what I had to believe, so I spent more and more time in my room meditating and playing a wood flute. The boys ridiculed me for it, but I just let them.

All the students came from affluent homes, but you would never know it from the food they fed us. Desserts were so scarce that Snickers candy bars were looked upon as a rare treat and became our barter to buy what we wanted from each other. We had to pay 2,500 Italian lira for one bar, which was twice as much as it would have been back home.

One day a boy named Eric dropped by my cabin. "Too bad we don't have some LSD, Doug," he said. "I'd just give anything for a little windowpane."

"Sorry, I don't have a thing," I told him, but after he left, my conniving mind went to work. LSD is called "windowpane" because it comes in small clear squares about an eighth of an inch on each side. I took a plastic picture holder from my wallet and snipped two tiny plastic squares. The finished product looked just like two hits of LSD windowpane.

The next time I saw Eric, I said, "You won't believe this, but I just happened to find a couple of hits of windowpane."

His eyes lighted up. "Great!" he said enthusiastically. "Will you sell me one? How much?"

"Well, I want two candy bars for one hit," I told him.

"It's a deal," he said. "I have them right here in my closet."

"Now wait a second, Eric. I don't know if this stuff is good anymore. It's been in my wallet a long time" (which was true, of course).

"Hey, it's OK." He waved my remark aside. "I'll take my chances." We made the exchange, and I turned to go.

"By the way, you have to swallow it," I cautioned him. "This kind doesn't melt in your mouth." Grinning, I went to my room and sat down on the edge of my bed. I tore the wrapper from the first candy bar and bit off a big chunk. I chewed slowly and savored the crunchy chocolate goo. "Umm, man! This will be long gone by the time he discovers he's eating my wallet," I chuckled.

Even though I had outsmarted him, a feeling of guilt nagged at me. "Oh, well," I rationalized, "he'd have done the same thing to me if he had thought of it."

I braced myself the next morning when he showed up at my door. "Now I'm going to get it," I thought.

He closed the door behind him, but he didn't look angry. In fact, he smiled. "You know that windowpane?" he said enthusiastically. "Well, at first nothing happened, and I just went to sleep, but then I woke up during the night, and man, what a trip! I was tripping and hallucinating all night!" He rolled his eyes and leaned back against my door.

My mouth must have dropped open. "Well, ah, what do you know!" I muttered. Later, when I discovered the Bible passage, "God bath dealt to every man a measure of faith," I thought of Eric. He sure had faith in that bit of plastic!

I had heard that there are no atheists in foxholes. I saw firsthand that there are no atheists in storms at sea, either. One evening we were skimming along at a pretty good clip off the coast of Sardinia when, within a matter of a few hours, the breeze turned into a howling fury and the choppy waves turned into great mountains of water twenty-five to thirty feet high. The bow rose high to meet the great waves, only to suddenly drop into the trough that followed, creating a violent rising and plunging motion that soon had the young seamen hanging onto rails and surrendering their supper to the sea. Many didn't make it to the rail, and the deck was soon strewn with the slippery filth as the poor boys heaved and vomited.

"Get away from that railing," the captain roared. "If anyone is swept overboard, we won't even turn around for you. You'd die of shock and cold before we could find you on a night like this. We'd just mark the map and show your parents where you died." This was probably a bluff, but we couldn't be sure.

Shipped Out!

As the fury of the storm increased, the waves broke over the bow of the ship, pouring tons of water onto the deck, and as the ship tipped up to meet the next wave, the water rolled aft, smashing everything in its path. Soon life jackets, boxes, and other debris bobbed and churned on the surface and swirled off the deck into the sea as the water rushed from bow to stern. The inflated life raft, secured precariously by a thread of rope, jerked about dangerously, threatening to join the mad rush.

"Quick, boys," the captain shouted at Ralph and me, the only two who were not laid low with seasickness. "Secure the life raft before another wave hits." Ralph, whose millionaire father lived in Virginia, was a big blond hillbilly—a rugged individualist. Another wave hit just as we reached the raft, sending us flying headlong into it. Our added weight snapped the string and propelled us down the deck of the ship on a foot of water. "Yee haw!" the hillbilly cried as we flew along, but I could see us heading straight for the railing, and my heart almost stopped. What if it didn't hold! It stopped us so suddenly that we almost flew over the sides, but we grabbed the railing and hung on desperately. Somehow we secured the raft and survived that crisis. But before we could congratulate ourselves, an even larger wave struck the ship, and the large mainsail ripped, leaving us dangerously crippled. If we lost our forward thrust, we could drift sideways and be hit broadside by the waves.

Everyone came running, sick or not, when they heard the rip. The sail started flapping violently in the shrieking gale. Many hands were needed to haul it down, unhook it, and hoist up the spare. We fought the ropes as the ship swayed, and the water pulled at our legs and tried to deck us, but we finally had the sail down and unhooked. I could see lips moving, and I knew some of my atheist friends were praying. We finally had the spare sail attached, ready to be hoisted to the top of the main mast. Someone would need to ride the saddle or ring to the top of the mast and secure it. Otherwise, as the boat rocked, the ring would dig into the mast and prevent it from sliding freely.

"We need someone to ride the saddle," the captain shouted over the wind. "Any volunteers?" He looked around with pleading eyes. I wasn't afraid of high places, and I knew I could do it if anybody could. I was still pretty strong from my days in military school.

"I'll go," I volunteered. I couldn't resist the temptation to show off.

I climbed onto the saddle, and the men and boys began to pull the winch. Slowly I was carried aloft. When it was about two-thirds of the way up, the boat rocked forty feet forward, and the ring started digging into the mast, making it impossible to raise it any farther. I pulled and pulled with all my strength, but I couldn't get the ring away from the mast. I could hear the ropes strain and groan as those below continued tightening, and I was afraid the ropes would snap.

"Stop! Stop! It's stuck," I shouted. I yelled again and again, but there was so much slack in the sail that it flapped violently in the wind, making a racket that sounded like thunder. Even though they were only twenty-five or thirty feet below me, they couldn't hear my shouts.

All this time, as the boat swayed dangerously from side to side, the tall mast swung in great arcs, almost dipping into the great waves on one side, then whipping me like a rocket through the air and almost dipping me into the waves on the other side. I knew if it rocked much farther I would fall off my perch and drown. My only hope was to jump from the saddle to the webbing that stretched from the side of the ship to the crow's nest. If I had been at the top, I could have just climbed directly from the mast onto the webbing, but since I was only two-thirds of the way up, the webbing was several feet out from the mast. My arms trembled from the exertion of trying to pull the ring out, and I knew there was barely any strength left in them. I also knew that if I jumped as we were tilted over the water, I could easily miss the webbing and plummet into the cold sea, and that would be the end of me.

"Oh, God! Save me, please," I cried. "Don't let me die!" With a quick glance below, I leaped. Thank God, my timing was right. I grabbed the webbing with my hands, hooked my legs through, and hung on for dear life. After resting a minute, I climbed down.

By this time the captain had discovered the problem and

had lowered the sail. My arms and legs still trembled as I stood and watched.

"Do you want to try again?" the captain asked.

"No way!" I said. "I'm going to my cabin." Carefully stepping over the debris that choked the hallway, I picked my way back to my quarters. I could hear the moaning and heaving of the other boys in their cabins. The stench of diesel and vomit gagged me as I reached my door. I hardly noticed the shambles the storm had made of my room. I collapsed onto my bunk and held to the bedrail. "I'm lucky to be alive!" I thought to myself. I wondered, as I lay there, how many prayers and promises had gone up to God that night. I also wondered how many of those who prayed would really change their lives if we lived through this storm.

Somehow, we did make it through. When we sailed in peaceful waters once again, life went on as usual. Everyone acted as though nothing had happened. All prayers and promises were forgotten. I learned that day why God doesn't discipline with fear. When the danger is past, people usually go back to their old ways.

Because I arrived at the school late, watch duty had already been assigned, and my name did not appear on the roster to stand watch. There were other assignments, however, including scrubbing the deck, washing dishes, and other chores that I hated. Finally I rebelled and refused to attend programs, go to class, or do any of the work assigned to me. I just sat in my room and meditated. Before long, the captain came banging on my door.

"It's open," I called.

He stormed in and began to rant and rave. "What's the meaning of this behavior, Batchelor? You aren't attending class. You aren't doing your work assignments. You aren't doing anything you're supposed to do. Don't you know you have to follow the rules like everyone else?"

"Why?" I asked belligerently. "I hate this place. I didn't ask to come here, and I'm not going to be a slave for anybody!" I did not feel intimidated by his angry words. I had a gold medal in wrestling and was used to fighting. I had never lost a match.

When he saw that he wasn't going to scare me, he changed his tactics. "OK, Batchelor, if you don't work, you don't eat!" he thundered. He turned on his heel and stormed off. I wondered what I would do, but I talked my roommates into smuggling food to me, and I continued in my defiance.

Morale began to break down among the other students. "Why do I have to stand watch? Batchelor doesn't." "Why do I have to scrub deck? Batchelor doesn't." The captain had no answer. At his wits' end, he came to see me again. "Batchelor, what do I have to do to get you to behave? You're destroying the morale of this school. Insubordination is spreading like a plague." His eyes looked at me beseechingly.

"I don't know." I shrugged. "Make me an offer."

"I'll tell you what. If you'll attend class and cooperate for a couple more weeks, I'll tell your dad you've been well-behaved and let you go home for Christmas."

I took a deep breath and thought a minute. "It's a deal," I agreed.

He knew that if I ever got off the boat I'd never be back. We both knew, but we didn't mention it. Of course, the first thing I did on the plane home for Christmas was to order a beer and a pack of cigarettes. While the other students looked on in horror, I told them, "You'll never see me again," and they didn't.

Dad was so delighted with the false report of my good behavior, I just couldn't spoil it by telling him the truth. Instead, I joined in the festivities of Christmas and tried to forget about school. But when it was time to return, I hit the road again.

8

On the Road

O h, brother, not another one!" I sighed as I pulled my light
jacket tighter to my body. A huge red-and-silver trac-
tor-trailer roared past. I counted "one, two, three," then
snapped around and turned my back to the icy blast. A cold gust
whistled down my neck, and I shivered for the hundredth time.
I glanced at my watch and began to walk again. Walking was
warmer than just standing with my thumb out.

"Almost eight hours in this miserable place, and it looks
like it might start snowing again," I muttered as my numb feet
dragged me along the shoulder of Interstate 40 on the outskirts
of a small Oklahoma town. My stomach growled, but I ignored
it as I turned to the approaching blue Cadillac and put out my
thumb. The driver didn't even glance my way. I shoved my hands
back into my pockets and began walking again.

Dark thoughts crowded into my throbbing head, and I
could hardly believe that only yesterday I had been in a toasty-
warm pool hall in Virginia, drinking, shooting pool with some of
my friends, and making stupid bets. The more I drank, the worse
I played, and soon I lost all my money. I could kick myself. "Why
didn't I save some money to eat on? What a fool I've been!" Did
I dare talk to God? I didn't have much training in praying, but I
knew God could read minds, so I prayed in my heart.

"God, I know I've been rotten. Forgive me for all the people
I've hurt, and please, send me a ride and something to eat and
some money. And while You're at it, please give me a ride all the
way to California—with somebody normal."

The first time I hitchhiked I was only five years old. Since

49

then I'd had some wild experiences hitchhiking. One man, who was smoking pot, went driving down the wrong side of the road into the traffic. Another time a couple were drunk and swerving all over the road. Finally I told them, "This is where I get off," even though it wasn't. I wanted to survive! Another time a man and his girlfriend who had been drinking picked me up. He thought he would impress us by turning off his lights as he drove and showing us he could drive in the dark. Sometimes homosexuals picked me up and tried to make bargains. On another occasion I found myself riding with a criminal, though I didn't realize it at the time. But the police pulled us over, handcuffed the guy, and hauled him away, leaving me standing there by an empty car with no keys. So I thought, while I was asking favors of God, that I had better ask for a ride with someone normal. I had hardly finished my little prayer when a white van pulled up and stopped.

"Where ya headed?" the driver asked cheerily.

"California," I told him.

"Praise the Lord! That's where I'm going. Hop in," he invited.

"Oh, no, a Jesus freak!" I thought to myself, but I gratefully climbed in beside him, and we were on our way. I was so glad to get a ride that I forgot all about the prayer I had just prayed until much later.

After a couple of comments about the cold weather, my benefactor glanced my direction. "I'll bet you've been visiting someone for Christmas and are headed home," he said.

"No, I've been living in Florida, but now I'm going out to California to live," I said evasively. "How about you?" I wasn't ready yet to discuss my plans with a stranger.

"Well, I'm going to find a friend in southern California. But tell me"—and he took his eyes off the road and looked right at me—"are you a Christian?"

His question startled me. I fancied myself very religious. I could talk about God, meditation, reincarnation, spiritual science, and the New Age movement. I was conversant on the subject of transmigration of the body and walking up walls. I had studied many Eastern religions. But when he asked if I were a Christian, I didn't know. Was he asking whether I believed the

Bible or whether I believed in loving others? Almost all religions teach that we should love others.

Seeing my bewilderment, he elaborated. "Do you believe in Jesus Christ?"

Again, I didn't know how to answer. I didn't know whether the story of Jesus was a fable, a fraud, a fairy tale, or whether He was just a nice teacher. We were soon discussing Jesus and the Bible and religion. It seemed like he preached to me all the way to California! In Colorado, the roads turned to ice. Cars were sliding off the road all around us. I could tell that he was not as frightened as I was. He just prayed aloud as he picked his way along. We did some sliding, but we never went off the road. I was impressed!

He bought all our meals and paid for our motel rooms. Later he picked up another hitchhiker. This young man turned out to be a Christian. I felt a little left out listening to them talk. He gave this young man $300 when he let him out!

As we approached California, he asked me, "Now where in California are you going?" Even though I hadn't appreciated the preaching, I felt real warmth toward this man who had been such a good friend, and I think I startled him by saying, "I'm going to some mountains near Palm Springs. I'm going to live in a cave in the San Jacinto Mountains."

I could feel his eyebrows raise, even though my eyes were looking straight ahead. "Who are you going to live with?"

"I'm not going to live with anyone; I'm going to live by myself," I answered almost defiantly.

"What are you talking about? You couldn't be more than seventeen." He sounded more curious than judgmental.

"I'm sixteen," I told him. "Anyhow, I've been on my own for years already. I'll be all right."

He took me right to the mouth of the canyon and handed me $40. As he pulled away, it struck me. Hey! God gave me all four things I prayed for that day in Oklahoma: a ride to California, food, and money—well, almost all four. I wasn't sure the guy was normal!

9

The Arabs Are Coming!

Before hiking up to the cave, I stopped at the store and went shopping with some of the $40 my kind friend had given me. But I didn't know much about meal planning for cave life. I bought several cans of food and some meat—heavy items for a backpack. After carefully stashing my purchases into my pack, I picked it up and struggled into the shoulder straps. I soon found the trail and left the town behind.

Remembering the steepness of the trail from the previous year, I walked slowly. Even though it was early January, the desert sun beat down, and before long, I stopped. I set the pack on the ground, peeled off my jacket, and stuffed it into the pack. After a brief rest, I shouldered my load again and resumed the path. I had determined to put as much distance as possible between me and people. I would go for the third valley.

I remembered trying to keep up with Jim and Sunny. That was child's play compared with this. Even without the jacket, I sweated like I was in a sauna. My body ached, and my breath came in gasps. The weight of the load pulling on the straps cut off the circulation, and my head began to ache. I felt like a tiny ant toiling up the bare boulders. Sometimes I took a wrong turn and walked a long way before discovering my mistake. I had made the trip only once before, and that was almost a year ago.

An hour dragged by, then two. I began to wonder if people ever died from being tired. Finally I stood atop the big ridge. Looking down, I could see Palm Springs 4,000 feet below me on one side and the third valley 1,500 feet down on the other side. As I surveyed the third valley, a huge, gray boulder arrested my attention. Nestled among the trees, it stood almost alone except for a smaller boulder behind it. Beyond the small boulder the sides of the mountains rose like a wall. From where I stood on the trail, it looked as though a stream ran right next to this massive rock. I decided to check it out. With renewed energy I took long, jolting strides down the trail into the valley.

When I reached the valley floor, I could see the top of the large boulder to my left, and I hiked toward it for about ten minutes. I scrambled over a large log between some rocks, and there it stood a few yards ahead of me. The sight of it took my breath away! At the base of the boulder a cave opened like an inverted bowl. The entrance, a shallow arch about thirty feet wide, gaped across the front, and sunlight flooded the interior. The creek flowed down the canyon to the right of the cave, hurried over a large, smooth boulder, and dropped into an emerald green pool about thirty feet across and ten feet deep. Sycamores and bay laurel crowded about. To the left stretched a level, grassy area that ended in a fringe of thicket. I walked toward the cave slowly, my eyes drinking in the beauty of the place.

Setting my backpack on the ground, I entered cautiously. I could see no signs of recent occupancy, but I could tell from the smoke-blackened ceiling that others had been here before me. The rock jutted out against one wall, forming a low shelf, and on the shelf lay a black book covered with an accumulation of dust. I picked it up and blew off the dust. *Holy Bible,* it said. I laid it down without even opening it. "Somebody else was looking for God," I said to myself. "They must not have found Him in this Bible, or they wouldn't have left it here."

Off to the left, behind a rock, I found another opening— a low one. I dropped to my knees and crawled through, and a moment later I was standing up in a low-ceilinged room. A little light shown in from the entrance, but it had a cozy feeling about it, like the inside of a bear's den. "What a good place to sleep!" I thought.

I could hardly wait to get set up. I wanted to stake claim to this little paradise right now! I went back outside, picked up my backpack, and took it into the first room. I took out my cans of food and placed them on a ledge. On the end of the ledge I put a neatly folded towel and a bar of soap. Then I took my sleeping bag and clothes and crawled into the "bedroom." Folding my clothes, I put them in a stack against the wall and rolled the sleeping bag out onto the floor. With my bedroom and kitchen ready, I fished my hammock out of the backpack and tied it between two sycamore trees beyond the pool.

Shadows already crept across the valley floor between the lofty walls of the canyon. The thought of being alone at night in this desolate place made me a little nervous. What if cougars and coyotes came to the pool to drink at night! I had better have a fire. Wild animals were afraid of fire—or so I thought. I found several smooth stones and laid them in a circle in the center of the cave, then went out to look for wood. I didn't stop until I had carried in several armloads and dropped them in a stack by my fire pit. Then I stood back and surveyed my new home. "Now I'm ready!" I said. It looked as tidy as my room awaiting inspection at the military academy!

In the weeks ahead I kept busier than I had thought possible. Cooking and cleaning took a good portion of my mornings. An old-timer in Palm Springs showed me how to make a stove from a large pot with a lid. I started each day by making banana bread for breakfast. There were dishes to wash, and there was food to hide from the little animals. I made a pot scrubber out of a ball of grass that grew by the stream. It worked as well as one from the store. I also made the pool by my cave two feet deeper by damming it where the water ran out. Every day there was something to work on.

I made a chair of logs and stones, complete with armrests and back, then covered it over with blankets. I could sit in comfort for hours at a time.

In the summer I peeled off my clothes and went natural. At first my bare feet were tender, and the sharp stones on the floor of my cave hurt them, so I dug them out. Then I carried up bucketfuls of sand from around the pool and made a smooth floor that felt good between my toes.

One of the things I made was an animal trap. I caught a squirrel, which I cooked and ate, and I made a pouch from the skin. I also killed a large rattlesnake, which I tried eating. It was mostly bones, so I ate only a little, but I made a sheath for my knife from its skin.

The Arabs Are Coming!

I had few ways of making money to supply my needs, but one project that gave me a little cash was making pipes, which I sold to a "head shop" in Palm Springs. Head shops dealt in pot pipes and other paraphernalia used by the drug culture.

At first I had to hike into town twice a week to do my shopping, but my shopping habits changed as I became more sophisticated in my new lifestyle, and I could get by with only once a week. I learned to buy dried foods like rice, spaghetti, beans, and flour.

Cooking rice and spaghetti posed no problem. They were always tender after fifteen or twenty minutes of boiling. But what a time I had with dried beans! The first time, I tried cooking them for fifteen minutes, but they were still as hard as rocks. I ate them anyway, but they made me sick. The next time, I doubled the cooking time to thirty minutes, but that didn't work much better. When they were still crunchy after an hour of boiling, I wondered if something was wrong with the beans. When I told a friend of my problem, he laughed and said, "You have to cook beans all day at this elevation."

Getting high and finding new ways of getting high had been almost the sole purpose of my existence, but now I began my search for God. One day I read a book about the American Indians' quest for God through hallucinatory plants, and I could hardly wait to try them for myself. One plant that had been mentioned in the book, called jimson weed, grew just a few yards from my cave. I picked some of the leaves and dried them, then rolled them into a cigarette. But there was no god there. After smoking the cigarette, all I got for my efforts was a dry mouth. Next I made a tea from the leaves, but again, I got a little dehydrated and that was all.

One day when I went to town for groceries, I ran into a hippie friend named Brad. After a little chitchat, I pulled a leaf from my pocket and showed it to him. "Do you know what this is?" I asked.

He reached for it, crushed it between his fingers, and sniffed. "Sure!" he said. "This is jimson weed. The Indians get high on it—part of their religion or something. It's high-powered stuff."

"No, it isn't," I replied. "I tried it. I smoked the leaves, and I made a tea, but nothing happened. It doesn't work."

Brad laughed. "You just don't know how it's done, man. I'll come up sometime and show ya." He had been to the cave on weekends a couple of times and knew where I lived.

A few days later, Brad, his brother Steve, and another young runaway named Mark showed up at the cave. "Are you ready for a trip?" he asked, after introducing his companions.

"Anytime you are," I said. He had brought a supply of the weed with him, and he showed me how to make a strong tea from the roots. He poured each of us a cup, but Steve declined.

"I'd better just watch," he said.

We all sat down on the floor of the cave and began to drink.

"Yuck! I never tasted anything so bitter!" I said.

"Good!" Brad laughed. "This will give us a real trip."

We waited a while, but nothing happened. "See! I told you it doesn't work."

"It'll work. Just give it time," Brad assured me.

"Let's go sunbathe by the pool," I suggested. They all liked the idea, and soon we were all stretched out in the sun. But a few minutes later I began to feel strange. "I'm going to bed," I said. I noticed my shoelace was untied and tried to tie it, but I couldn't make my fingers work. I gave up and stumbled into the cave, threw up, and passed out on the floor.

When I awoke, it was dark outside. I lighted a candle. First I noticed a Coke machine in my cave. "Good!" I thought. "My mouth feels dry, and I really need a drink." But I was interrupted by a voice.

"Where are you going, Doug? Come here, come here." I turned and saw my grandmother standing by a gray van. "Get into the van, get into the van!" she ordered in a shrill voice. I tried to open the van, but it turned into a rock. The next thing I knew I found myself out on the hillside, surrounded by pygmies who were coming after me with bows and arrows. I scrambled up the hillside as fast as I could go.

"Help! Help!" I screamed as I struggled to reach my friends back at the cave. "Help me! They're going to kill me!" When I finally made it to the cave, I found my friends dead, floating in the pool. (Actually, they were miles away in Palm Springs.)

The sun had gone down, but the moon had risen, and I

could see figures crouched, ready to spring at me. I screamed and kicked at them and began running down the mountains. (The crouched figures were actually cactus. You can guess how I found out!) But instead of keeping to the trail, I cut across, taking the most direct route to Palm Springs. Why I didn't kill myself, I cannot explain, except that God must have had His hand over me, even then. My descent was so steep and I had so much adrenaline pumping through my veins that I took giant leaps. Each step seemed like about thirty feet, though I'm not sure to this day whether that was reality.

I glanced over my shoulder and saw tanks rumbling down the mountainside toward me. Arabs swarmed after them carrying rifles. It all seemed so real. I never experienced so much fear in my life.

It was after two o'clock in the morning when I finally reached level land near Palm Springs. In the distance I saw light shining from a bar and ran toward it. It was closed, but I could hear voices inside. "Let me in, let me in!" I screamed, banging on the door with my fist. "They're after me! They're going to kill me!"

The door opened, and two wide-eyed black men pulled me inside and locked the door. "I don't see anybody," one of them said. "Who's going to kill you?"

"Where's the phone? I have to call the police!" I gasped, ignoring the man's question. They both pointed to a pay phone at one end of the bar. I dialed the emergency number, and a voice answered immediately.

"My name is Doug Batchelor!" I yelled into the phone. "I'm from a cave up in the mountains, and the Arabs are after me. They've already killed my friends!"

The voice at the other end was silent just a split second. "Where are you?" he asked.

"I'm at a bar. Wait! I'll find out," I said. I turned to the two men, who stood at my elbow, watching with concern. "Where are we?" I asked. They quickly repeated the address in unison, and I relayed it to the man on the other end.

"We'll be right there," he said.

In about two minutes a police car screeched to a stop in front of the bar, and two policemen jumped out and came hurrying inside. I met them, wild-eyed. One stepped in front of me, sniffed my breath, and shone a light in my eyes. "No marijuana, no alcohol," he reported to the other officer. "Come on over to the police station," he said, and opened the door for me. He climbed into the back seat, and the other officer slid in behind the steering wheel.

At the police station they took me through a side door. Once again they checked for any odor of drugs and frisked me, but they found nothing to indicate drugs. Except for being badly frightened, I appeared to be normal. They talked together in low voices, but with ears made acute from mountain living, I heard every word.

"What do you think?" one said in worried tones. "Do you think this has anything to do with the oil embargo?"

"Could be," the other officer answered. The sergeant opened another door and summoned a third officer. "This is top secret," he said in a low voice. "You'd better come in and take this down." The officer came in and inserted some paper into the typewriter. It clattered away as we talked. He could type faster than anyone I ever saw. He had no trouble keeping up with our speech. The sergeant turned to me. "Now, tell us exactly what happened."

I decided to leave out the part about the pygmies who were after me with bows and arrows. Somehow that didn't fit anymore. "Well, I was in my cave," I began. "I heard shots. I went outside, and I saw a bunch of people coming after me."

"Could you see what they looked like?" the sergeant asked.

"Not very well."

"Did you say they were Arabs? What did they look like? How could you tell they were Arabs?" he asked.

"The moon was shining, and I could see their headdresses and their robes. They were Arabs, all right."

The other officer broke in, speaking rapidly under his breath, but again I could hear him well. "The Arabs are mad about the oil embargo. They must be planning to attack Palm Springs!" All three men looked worried. The President had a home there, and many wealthy and famous people lived in Palm Springs, so they took every report seriously.

"You said they killed your friends. Were they shooting at you?" he asked.

"Oh, yes. There were people all over the place. They were shooting at me, and I was running straight down the mountains." I showed them my torn boots riddled with cactus. "Then these big boulders turned into tanks and came rumbling down the mountainside toward Palm Springs."

The typing slowed down and stopped, and the men looked sheepishly at one another. Finally, one of them spoke. "You must be on something—we're not sure what, but you're under age, and we're going to lock you up for a few days." With that, he walked to the telephone and called someone at the juvenile department to come over and get me.

10

New Mexico and Back

I spent two days at the Palm Springs jail with only doughnuts and coffee for food before someone came to transport me to the Riverside County Youth Center (a nice name for junior jail). It took two days for me to stop "seeing things" and realize that I had just had a bad "trip."

I couldn't help wondering what they would do with me at juvenile hall. I thought of the mess I had made of things with Dad in Florida. I couldn't blame him if he never wanted to see me again. Little did I realize that even while I sat in jail, he was working in my behalf, trying to find a solution to this problem. Going back to Mom was out of the question. I could think of only one solution—to escape and head for my cave.

In Riverside my cellmate (also named Doug) and I began to plan. We smuggled in some matches, and one of us melted the plastic around the bolts that held the plexiglass panes in the window while the other watched for the guard. We looked at each other jubilantly but silently when, after six packs of matches, the last bolt gave way. I removed the pane carefully and looked out. No one was about, but I could hear voices coming from down the hall, so I quickly snapped it back into place. We surveyed our work with satisfaction. The marks and burns were hard to see, and no one would suspect that the window had been tampered with. We decided to wait for the right time to make our getaway.

Before we had a chance to carry out the rest of the plan, though, an officer came and unlocked the door. "Doug Batchelor!"

"Yeah," I replied.

"Come with me," he ordered. "We are releasing you into the custody of your uncle, Harry Batchelor, in New Mexico."

I could hardly believe my ears. Uncle Harry operated an Indian trading post on a Navajo reservation. He and Aunt Nita were two of the nicest people I knew. He loved the Navajos and did not exploit them like some of the Indian traders. His honesty and fairness were proverbial among the Indians, and he helped them in every way possible. He made no claims to being a Christian, but in many ways he lived like one.

"Your uncle will pick you up at the airport," the officer said.

I felt relieved. "Uncle Harry won't be sorry," I resolved. "I'll be the best help he ever had."

And I did help at first. Uncle Harry and Aunt Nita treated me like their own son. My cousin Donnie was about my age, and we hit it off well. I could feel the love of the whole family and their genuine concern for my welfare. For the first time since military school, I really felt good about myself.

My uncle had two stores, and I worked at the one in Kimbito, New Mexico. I stocked the shelves, swept the floors, and kept the place tidy. "Help yourself to whatever you want, Doug," my uncle would say. He really didn't mind that I took cigarettes. He himself smoked and didn't object to my smoking. I helped myself to a sandwich when I got hungry and to ammunition when Donnie and I went out on the open range for target practice.

I liked the Navajos, especially the girls. Few of the young people among them showed interest in school or leaving the reservation, but there were exceptions. One day a good-looking eighteen-year-old came into the store. I could tell by his bright eyes and intelligent conversation that he was no ordinary young man. "I've never seen you before," I said as I waited on him. "Where are you from? What's your name?"

"My name is Ken Platero. I live here on the reservation, but I go to school at a college in Washington." He smiled rather shyly. "I'm home on spring break," he explained.

I was impressed. "Boy, you must be smart!" I said. "Is your old man rich?"

"Naw, I'm attending on a scholarship," he said as he picked up his bag.

"Why don't you drop by sometime after the store closes, and we'll ride motorcycles," I invited. He liked my outgoing ways, and I admired his intelligence and good looks.

I didn't realize what a desperate problem alcoholism is among the Indians. Due to something in their physical makeup, they become alcoholics more easily than most people. My uncle told me that in all of his years at the reservation he had never met an Indian who could take a drink, put the lid on the bottle, and put it away. "They drink until they are out of money, out of drink, or passed out," he said.

A few days after I met Ken, we went riding. Ignoring my uncle's wisdom, I made a foolish suggestion that I have regretted ever since. "Let's go down to the bar and get a sixpack," I said. I wanted a drink, and I gave no thought to the consequences.

Ken's whole expression changed. His eyes dropped as though ashamed, but he said, "Naw, Doug. Drinking is bad news. I don't want any part of it."

Unfortunately, I persisted. "Aw, come on, Ken. One drink won't hurt. Anyhow, I'm not old enough to buy it myself." I had not yet turned seventeen.

"Naw, Doug. I don't want to get started with that. Drinking is trouble. Everybody who drinks has trouble."

I could see the struggle. His common sense said No, but his natural courtesy and desire to please said Yes. Finally, he consented. I handed him some money. We climbed onto our bikes, and we roared down the road to the bar. He went inside and returned minutes later with a six-pack. I shoved the package inside my jacket and zipped it up. Then we headed for open country and finished off the beer together.

A day or two later we did the same thing, only this time it took less urging on my part. Before the week was over, we had not only visited the bar several times, but I had also taught him how to make his own beer in a five-gallon water bottle with yeast and malt syrup. Poor Ken! He never made it back to his college.

I began to spend less time working in the store and more time riding the motorcycle, drinking, chasing girls, and getting into trouble. As I got more and more out of control, my unhappiness grew.

Finally, Uncle Harry called me in and talked to me. "Doug,"

he said seriously, "if you want to be part of the family, you're going to have to behave yourself. Otherwise, you have to go." I never saw my uncle look so sad, and I felt terrible. A few days later I hocked my watch for twenty dollars, bought a new backpack, and hitchhiked back to my cave in California. I had blown it again!

I stopped in Palm Springs and bought supplies before heading for the cave. I had just left the market when I heard someone call my name.

"Hey, Doug!"

I turned around, and there stood Jim looking at me intently. This was the same Jim who had shown me his cave in Tahquitz Canyon when I was fifteen.

"Is that really you, Batchelor?" He shook his head in disbelief.

"Yeah, it's me, all right," I assured him. "I just got back from an Indian reservation in New Mexico."

Apparently Jim had heard about me again through the friends who introduced me to jimson weed. "We all thought you were dead," he said with a grin. "We didn't see you after that jimson-weed party at your cave. We looked for your body for days and finally gave up. I'm glad you're still around."

"Thanks," I mumbled. The whole affair flashed into my mind again, and I felt embarrassed as I thought of the fool I had made of myself. "How did the others make out?" I asked with some concern.

"Not too well," Jim said. "Mark walked through some hot coals and burned his feet so badly he ended up in the hospital, but he's out now." He seemed reluctant to go on.

"How about Brad? What happened to him?" I persisted.

Jim just shook his head. After a long pause, he said, "No one really knows. Steve told me that after you guys passed out he stretched out on the floor in the cave and went to sleep. When he woke up the next morning, everyone was gone. Brad may very well be at the bottom of the canyon somewhere."

No wonder they thought I was dead too! I thought sadly of my wild flight down the mountain that night and wondered again how I ever came out alive.

I did a lot of serious thinking as I climbed the path back

to my cave that day. No matter how much I tried to rationalize my feelings, I couldn't escape the conviction that I not only hurt myself when I did wrong, but I also hurt others around me. Did my foolishness cost Brad his life? During that whole climb up the mountain to my cave, guilt weighed down on me more than the pack on my back.

I finally reached the third valley. Leaving the trail, I turned toward the cave, and stopped dead in my tracks. Coming around a large boulder in the path, I almost ran head-on into a young man. Momentarily startled, we both stopped and looked at each other. "Howdy," I said at last. "Name's Doug."

"I'm Glen," he answered. We nodded to each other.

"Whatcha doin' up here?" I asked.

"I live here."

"Where at?"

"My cave," he answered timidly. He jerked a thumb over his shoulder, indicating somewhere behind him.

"Do you know Jim and Sunny?" I asked.

"Yeah."

To myself, I thought, "What's wrong with this guy? Doesn't he know how to talk?"

By now it was obvious that he enjoyed his little game of one question at a time, so I grinned.

"Well, I've come back up here to live. My place is that big cave under the boulder." I pointed to the prominent rock ahead.

I studied him carefully as I talked to him. He was a small man, about five feet, seven inches tall, with a scruffy beard and penetrating brown eyes. Even though he appeared to be about twenty-five years old, his light brown hair was thin on top and receded a little. His skin had grown dark from his outdoor living. Something about this character intrigued me. His reluctance to talk gave me the impression that he hoarded some secret, and I wondered what it was. Later I learned that his parents had been medical missionaries to India. The people and the schools in India were so different that when the family moved back to America it took some adjusting. He felt uncomfortable around American kids and kept largely to himself. In spite of his great intellect and talents, he had never married. Now he seemed to be running away from life.

New Mexico and Back

As it turned out, the two of us were the only occupants of this valley and would be for the next few months. He liked my talkative ways, and I was intrigued by his mysterious quietness. However, for now, we said goodbye to each other with a promise to visit each other soon.

When I arrived back at my cave, I wasn't surprised to find that my supplies had disappeared. After all, I had been in New Mexico for three months, and my friends thought I was dead. What did surprise me was that the Bible was still lying there where I had put it. A voice said, "Pick it up and read it, Doug," but I stifled the voice and decided to read it later. First, I had to fix the place up again.

I hummed as I put away my supplies. The music of the water gurgled like happy children chattering among themselves. The sun shone overhead, a breeze whispered among the sycamore trees, and a linnet outside sang cheerily. I was home!

One afternoon as I sat in my cave and rolled a cigarette, I heard a faint "meow." I sat still and cocked my head to listen.

"Meow."

Sure enough, it sounded like a cat. There were bobcats and mountain lions up here, but this was a cat-cat. How would a kitty cat get way up here in these desert mountains, I wondered? Then I saw it. Hopping over the rocks across the creek was the most beautiful black-and-white cat with long Persian fur.

"Where did you come from?" I asked.

I never found out the answer to that question, but for the next year and a half, "Stranger" made himself at home in my cave. He was a fierce hunter and would supply a good part of his own food by catching squirrels, birds, and, of course, mice. None of these creatures lasted long in my cave after Stranger arrived.

Sometimes at night, when he had finished hunting, he would hop up in my bedroom cave and gently push my nose with his paw until I lifted the blankets. Then he would crawl down to my feet and curl up and purr. I confess that it was a very relaxing sensation for me, but once, when he had lost an argument with a skunk, I had to evict him for a week.

I spent many happy hours exploring my canyon and the surrounding country until I knew it like the back of my hand. From spring till fall, hiking enthusiasts would come up on weekends and frequently stopped by to ask directions or to sit and talk.

One day Glen and I were hiking out of the canyon to town, when suddenly we heard a moaning sound. Looking over a nearby ledge, we saw a young man sitting on the edge of a rock, groaning and shaking. Blood oozed from a gash in his scalp and ran down one side of his face. His clothes were torn and his body covered with scrapes, bruises, and dried blood. We hurried down to him.

"What happened?" I gasped. He continued to groan and rock back and forth, but did not answer. Apparently he was in shock and oblivious to our presence.

Glen glanced up. "Looks like he fell from up there." He pointed to the ridge a hundred feet above us. "I don't know why the fall didn't kill him."

"We'd better go for help!" I said. I leaned over and put my face close to the man's ear. "We'll be back, man. Just hang in there!" Glen and I took off down the trail toward Palm Springs, and I'm sure we broke a record for getting off that mountain.

At the Mayfair Market we phoned the Search and Rescue office. "Quick!" I gasped. "There's a man hurt badly up in Tahquitz Canyon. He fell off the trail. He's hurt badly!"

After a few hurried exchanges of questions and answers, they told me they would send out a two-man team in a helicopter right away. We hurried back up the trail to stay with the injured man and to flag the helicopter and show the paramedics where to go.

The chopper found a place to hover. Two men scrambled out and hurried over with their equipment, while the pilot kept the engine running.

Glen and I stood and watched. The paramedics quickly took the man's vital signs, started an IV, and strapped him onto a stretcher.

There was no flat area for the helicopter to land, so the skilled pilot rested one runner on the edge of a little cliff. The four of us carried the injured man slowly up the rocky hillside to the chopper. The poor fellow groaned every time our feet slipped. As we neared the chopper, I became concerned for my own safety. The rotating blades churned the air about us, and dust and cactus balls tumbled about everywhere in the swirling dust. It was easy to see that if the small rock the chopper rested on gave way, it would drop on us and turn us into hamburger. But we soon had the injured man fastened down securely, and the whirlybird rose and soared off to the hospital.

Later I ran into the helicopter pilot in town, and he told me that the young man had been drinking when he fell. "He was lucky you two came along when you did," the pilot said.

I felt good about helping with a rescue. That marked the beginning of my friendship with the Riverside Search and Rescue team. Lost and injured hikers were all too common in those rugged mountains. On many occasions the helicopter team would fly low over my cave and ask me, by way of a bullhorn, if I had seen a hiker. I would answer with gestures or by waving a red towel. Although I was a trespasser—for this was a reservation for the Agua Caliente Indians—no one bothered me because of my cooperation with the Search and Rescue team.

Most of the people who fell had been drinking or using drugs. Not all of the victims had happy endings. Walking along a narrow cliff trail watching their footing, hikers would forget the high backpack that stuck up behind them. Every now and then a pack would bump into overhanging rocks, and the bump would send them hurtling into the canyon below.

Some hikers tried following a creek down the mountain and ended up in a deathrap. A series of three pools at the bottom of the third valley lured them. In order to reach the first pool, they had to slide down a steep, almost vertical wall. Farther down the creek they came to the second pool, also at the bottom of a steep-sided boulder. As they saw the third pool they continued their journey downward. What they could not see was the 100-foot waterfall below the third pool. By the time they reached that point, they were trapped. Without special equipment, there was no way out. Trying to climb back up would be much like a beetle trying to climb up the inside of a glass jar. Some died of exposure. Others starved or died of snakebite, and one older man died of a heart attack after falling into the cold water of the pool.

When I went shopping in town, I was appalled at the street people who dug in dumpsters behind the food markets. "Watcha doin'?" I asked the first time I saw them.

"Oh, we're treasure hunting. The stores throw away a lot of good stuff, especially bananas."

"Yuck!" I thought to myself. "I would never take food from such a stinky spot. Those people have no self-respect."

Every time I came to town, I saw these people rummaging through the garbage. Finally I grew curious enough that I edged closer. Soon I was pointing out things I could see, and before long I, too, was rooting through the garbage with the best of them. My favorite finds were the brown-freckled bananas that were too ripe for the stores to sell, but just right for making my banana bread. We found lots of bread and pizza behind a bakery called Nicolino's. Instead of selling it as day-old, they threw it away, and we could always find a good supply. Later, when I became a Christian, I thought, "Sin is like digging in the garbage! At first it seems odious and distasteful, but as you become more accustomed to it, it seems less so, and finally you're in it all the way."

I soon became friends with the street people in Palm Springs. None of them had normal names like Bob or Jim. They all had nicknames like Crazy Dan, Railroad, or Pack Rat. One day a friend named Rico was teasing me among some of our buddies. "You're a cave man," he said. "We can't call you Doug anymore. We'll call you Duh-ugh. Yep. That's the first word ever spoken by a caveman. Duh-ugh."

"I'd much prefer being plain Doug, or even 'cave man,'" I said. "But not Duh-ugh."

So they called me Cave Man, and the name is still with me among these friends.

The street people had some comical ways. Little Richie, a young man about four feet, ten inches high, would sleep in a Good Will drop box at night. He was just small enough to fit through the trapdoor, and he liked sleeping there because the old clothes people threw in made a nice, soft bed. But early one morning before Richie woke up, someone decided to donate their old pots and pans to Good Will. You can imagine Richie's surprise when pots and pans began clattering down on his head. And you can imagine the donor's surprise when he heard, "Hey, cut it out!" echoing from the drop box!

Then there was Crazy Dan. He had blown his mind on LSD and would argue with the mannequins in the store windows.

New Mexico and Back

I could play a recorder when I first moved to the cave, but recorders are somewhat limited, and I found myself wishing for something more versatile. When my brother wrote and asked what I wanted for my birthday, I asked for a flute.

A few weeks later a package arrived. I opened it eagerly, and there lay a beautiful new silver Yamaha flute in a fine blue-velvet case. Learning to play turned out to be harder than I thought, but I had plenty of time, and eventually I could play well enough to make people think I knew what I was doing. When I went to town to shop after that, I took my flute along. I would find a good spot in front of the bookstore where other hippies hung out and would sit down cross-legged on the walk and play my flute. Occasionally passersby would stop and listen, and sometimes drop coins into the cup I had sitting in front of me. When I thought I had collected enough to do my shopping, I would scoop up my take and head for the Mayfair Market to buy the items the dumpsters failed to provide.

11

Discovering the Truth

The novelty of cave life eventually wore off, and not much was happening. Surrounded by the grandeur of nature, my thoughts turned more to God. I longed for that elusive inner peace that had brought me to this place in the beginning, and I spent a lot of time with books on philosophy and Eastern religions. The Eastern religions told me to meditate, to look within, because there I would find God. But the more I looked within, the more dissatisfied I became, for I knew that on the inside I was a mess.

My mind had been biased against the Christian religion by my Jewish relatives, who, of course, did not accept Jesus as the Messiah. I had been told that Christianity was the cause of all the wars of European history—the crusades, the massacres of the Dark Ages, and the wars in Ireland between Catholics and Protestants.

One thing I had heard about Jesus Christ did intrigue me, though. I had been told, erroneously, that He taught reincarnation. I decided to look into that. I might even find ammunition to use against the Jesus freaks who liked to argue religion with me.

One day I took the Bible down from the rock shelf and wiped off the dust. It said, "Holy Bible, King James Version." I wondered who King James's "virgin" was, for even though I had finished the ninth grade I was not a fluent reader, and I misread the word. Opening the Bible to the inside cover, I found a handwritten message: "Born again July 12, 1972. It is my prayer that whoever finds this Bible will read it and find

70

the peace and joy that I found." Below that was my benefactor's signature.

"Well," I thought, "I'm looking for peace, all right, but I doubt that I'll find it here." Nevertheless, I sat down on my chair and began to read. Every time I came to the word *brethren*, I thought it said *breathing*. "This must be some spiritual term," I thought. You'd be amazed how much breathing they do in the book of Acts!

Even though I struggled with the King James's outdated language, the stories captivated me. It seemed that a divine presence stood by my side, impressing me that this was truth. I liked the story of Adam and Eve and wished that I could believe it, because it would help me to feel better about myself. If God created the first man and woman, that made me a descendent of a son of God, not a descendent of some amoeba or monkey! As I read on I found myself reliving those early events. It saddened me that Adam and Eve disobeyed and had to leave the Garden of Eden.

The story of the Flood gripped my imagination. If water had covered the whole earth, no wonder I had found fossils of sea life at 7,000 feet when I lived in New Mexico. It also explained why the walls of my canyon were worn smooth hundreds of feet high. A catastrophic flood carrying tons of silt as it surged back and forth made more sense than anything my teachers had taught me in school.

When my chair became too hard, I got up and went to my hammock and continued reading. When hunger pangs began to gnaw at my stomach, I reluctantly laid the Bible down and fixed myself a lunch. Then I sat down before my "table" (an overturned bucket), laid the Bible on my knee, and continued to read between bites.

Jacob reminded me of myself. His deceitful trick got him in trouble at home, forcing him to flee for his life. I thought of all the times I had run away from home. The part where he finally returned to his father nearly brought tears to my eyes.

I read and reread the Ten Commandments. They seemed to be such a perfect set of rules! I noticed that the fourth commandment said to keep holy the seventh day, so I looked at an old calender in my bedroom cave. "Isn't that Saturday?" I wondered. Then I read the commandments a third time. "If people would just live by these rules, how different our world would be!" I thought.

I began to bog down when I got into the latter part of Exodus with all the names I couldn't pronounce, and I finally laid the Bible aside, but my mind continued playing those stories back to me, and I began to realize that God *did* concern Himself with human affairs.

One day I ran into a Jesus freak in town, but instead of avoiding him as I usually did, I told him I had been reading the Bible. "But the stories ended," I said sadly. "From there on, it's all names and numbers, and it keeps repeating the same stuff. Aren't there any more good stories?"

"Sure, the Bible is full of them," he replied. "Why don't you try the New Testament? Matthew, Mark, Luke, and John. They're all about Jesus Christ."

"I'm not sure I believe in Jesus Christ," I said slowly.

He didn't argue. "It's up to you," he said.

I decided that I would try the New Testament. Matthew started out with a genealogy, and I began to think I had made a mistake, but I soon got out of the "begats" and was happy to find that the story had a plot after all. I really had my guard up when I began Matthew, but instead of finding Jesus to be a deceiving charlatan seeking glory for Himself, I found Him to be a warm, powerful, caring, forgiving person who went about teaching people, healing them, and raising them from the dead.

I felt a divine presence assuring me that this was truth, but Satan still hung around creating doubt. "You don't even know that such a person even existed. Maybe He's just a fantasy invented by clever writers!" he whispered.

Well, maybe, but I'd check and see what I could find out. I visited the public library in Palm Springs. I learned that not only was Jesus a historical figure; He was so important that all history is calculated from the date of His birth!

I finished reading Matthew and started on Mark, who told much the same story, but it seemed more action packed. I really loved the book of Luke, especially the story of the Prodigal Son. I felt that I was that rebellious son who needed to turn to my heavenly Father.

Luke also told the story of the Good Samaritan. I thought of all the people who had passed me by when I was down and out hitchhiking. Then that Christian came along, like the Samaritan, and helped me. I began to see Christianity in a new light, and all other religions paled in comparison. Instead of telling me to look inward for strength, it told me to look to Jesus. He would give me the rest and forgiveness I was searching for.

The book of John, with its profound concepts of God and His love, thrilled me, and I could feel Jesus drawing me.

By the time I finished the four Gospels, I knew I had to decide what to do about Jesus. I knew He really lived, but who was He? I could see three options. Either He was crazy, He was a liar, or He was who He claimed to be, the Son of God.

I wanted with all my heart to know the truth. It didn't occur to me that I could pray for guidance, but I'm sure God understood the longing of my heart and helped me to think it through.

"Could He have been crazy?" I asked myself.

I thought of the many times He had silenced His enemies by just a few words. I thought of the power of His words, like the Sermon on the Mount, and how He read the thoughts and intentions of people's hearts. No, I decided, He was not crazy. He was brilliant.

"Was He a liar and a deceiver?"

I thought of His life of unselfish ministry, how He went about healing the sick, raising the dead, and casting out demons. He devoted His entire life to promoting truth and exposing hypocrisy. Had He been a liar, He could easily have lied at His trial and escaped death. I was a terrific liar, and they say it takes one to know one. No, He was not a liar.

That left only one conclusion.

Jesus had to be who He claimed to be—God made flesh and come to earth to dwell among us. As this realization dawned upon me, I fell to my knees right there on the floor of my cave. "Lord Jesus!" I cried aloud. "I believe that You are the Son of God and my Saviour. I believe that You paid for my sins. I want You to come into my life and show me how to follow You."

Satan hastened to discourage me in the step I was taking.

I could actually feel the forces of good and evil punching it out in my heart.

"What are you doing?" Satan asked. "You've been up here too long. Here you are, talking to yourself! Anyhow, you're a hopeless sinner. Remember all the wicked things you have done? You've gone too far."

"But what have I got to lose, except my sin and guilt?" I answered. "Jesus, I know I've done a lot of mean, stupid things. I'm sorry. Will You please forgive all of them? And will You please change me?"

I remained on my knees a little longer. I didn't feel lightning or anything dramatic, but somehow I *knew* that God heard my prayer and forgave my sins. My heart began to fill with the sweetest peace I had ever experienced. Slowly I rose to my feet and looked about. The whole world seemed more beautiful. The music of the waterfall, the clear water of my pool, the swaying trees, the blue sky—what a wonderful world God had made for people to live in! My heart sang, and I longed to share my happiness with someone.

I didn't quit smoking that day. I didn't quit drinking, nor did I stop smoking pot. God didn't overwhelm me by showing me all the changes I would need to make in my life, but He did accept me, and I knew that I belonged to Christ. The Holy Spirit would convict me of my sins one by one as I grew in grace.

A couple of days later a Baptist guy came hiking by my cave and stopped to chat. Immediately our conversation turned to religion, and I told him all about my surrender to Jesus. "That's great, Doug! I'm so happy for you," he said sincerely, "but you haven't been baptized, have you?"

"Why, no," I admitted slowly. "I hadn't even thought about it. Where does it say that?" He took my Bible and quickly turned to the book of Matthew. "Here it is, Matthew 28:19: 'Go ye therefore, and teach all nations, baptizing them in the name of the Father, and of the Son, and of the Holy Ghost.'"

"Well, I guess that's plain enough," I admitted, "but how can I be baptized? I don't even know a preacher."

"That's no problem," he said. "Here's water. I'll baptize you."

"Well, uh . . ." I hesitated. "OK! If that's what I'm supposed to do, let's do it. I'll get something to dry off with." I took two towels from my shelf and laid them on the ground beside the pool. We both gasped as we stepped into the ice-cold water.

"Hold on to my left wrist," he said. I grasped it with both hands. He raised his right hand above my head and said solemnly, "Brother Doug, because of your faith in Jesus Christ as the Son of God, I now baptize you in the name of the Father, and of the Son, and of the Holy Ghost. Amen." He lowered me into the water, then raised me up. We both scrambled out of that cold water, but I felt ecstatic as we dried our dripping bodies.

My ecstasy was short-lived, though. Later that day I hiked to town to celebrate my baptism with a couple of beers. Something inside said, "No, Doug, Christians don't drink."

"But didn't Jesus drink wine?" I reasoned. "Didn't He turn water into wine?" I had not been taught that in the Bible the word *wine* often means "grape juice." Sometimes, when it was fermented, it was called "mixed wine" or "strong drink." Later I was to discover that in reality, the Bible taught that drinking is foolish and wicked (see Proverbs 20:1).

I had used many drugs in my life, including LSD, hash, uppers, downers, THC, PCP, and cocaine, but none of these drugs was more addicting or dangerous than alcohol. More than half of the highway deaths are caused by alcohol, and more than half the people in prisons, hospitals, and mental institutions are there because of alcohol.

I didn't plan to get drunk that day, but after one beer, my willpower was weakened, so I had some more with a friend, and before the sun went down on my baptism I was arrested for public misconduct.

My Baptist friend had overlooked the important next verse. "Go ye therefore, and teach all nations, baptizing them in the name of the Father, and of the Son, and of the Holy Ghost: *teaching* them to observe all things whatsoever I have commanded you." He hadn't taught me how to live the Christian life. In his defense I will say that teaching a new Christian takes a lot of time, and he was just hiking by my cave that day. God used him to start me on my Christian walk. Later, other Christians taught me how to live the Christian life.

I felt ashamed when I was released from jail the next day,

but somehow I knew that God would forgive me, and I continued to read and pray. I began to watch for signs that the Lord was with me. I read in Scripture, "Give thanks always." I took God at His word. If I bumped my head or hurt myself in some way, I said "Thank You, Lord." I didn't want to let the devil make me curse, and I knew that I couldn't thank God and curse at the same time.

I felt disappointed that Glen seemed uninterested in my new happiness. I couldn't understand his attitude, but I didn't let this dampen my spirits. My enthusiasm grew daily, and I began to pray that God would open a way for me to witness for Him. "But that might be too hard, even for God," I thought. "There's no one up here except Glen, and he doesn't want to listen."

Little did I suspect what God had in store for me—or for Glen! I didn't realize at the time that Glen was interested in spiritual things, but a few years later, he recommitted his life to God.

12

Star for a Day

A few days after I had prayed that God would show me how I could witness for Him, I hiked out of the canyon to make my monthly phone call to my mother. She sounded excited when she heard my voice.

"Oh, Doug, guess what!" she bubbled. "I was having lunch with this TV news reporter from CBS, and he thought that something about a millionaire's son living in a cave would make a good human interest story. He wants to come up and do it."

"Great," I said. Being on TV sounded exciting. I guess I inherited some of Mom's love of the theatrical. "When are they coming?" I asked.

"I don't know. Call me tomorrow. I should know by then," she said. I made the long hike out and back several times that week, but it was always the same, "Call back tomorrow."

Finally, in her frustration with CBS, Mom contacted NBC. They jumped at the story. At 9:30 the next morning I met my mother and *two* television crews, CBS's and NBC's. Both crews had unwittingly boarded the same plane and arrived at the airport together. A loud argument erupted immediately over who would get the story. It was all very embarrassing to me. Mom, bless her heart, waded right in and acted as referee.

"You had your chance," she told the CBS men. "My son kept making trips down and back every day, and you just kept us dangling. We're giving the story to NBC."

The CBS man grew red in the face and began yelling at Mom. "Don't you realize, lady, that it takes a lot of work to set something like this up? This was the soonest I could get all the arrangements made," he sputtered.

"That may be, but it sure didn't take NBC long to get it together," she countered. "They get the story, and that's that!"

"Do you have any idea how much money this is costing my company? Madam, you are despicable!" With that, he took his crew and stormed off.

At first I wondered, "Lord, why did it all have to happen this way?" Later I learned that the CBS newsman had brought along a pair of leopard Tarzan shorts to wear, and he planned to make a comedy of the whole thing. God knew all along what He was doing!

The flap didn't bother Mom, though. She had things organized in short order, and we started moving out. Our helicopter pilot, Pete Scott, had to make two trips to get everyone up to the third canyon, but it didn't take long in a chopper.

What a thrill to see the trail I had hiked over so many times from the air! It took a great deal of skill to land. There was no room to land in front of the cave, so Pete found a large boulder down canyon that was flat enough to rest one runner on, and he hovered while the passengers got themselves and their equipment off.

Pete and I knew each other pretty well. He was the same Pete who worked on the Search and Rescue team, and he always checked with me when searching for a lost hiker. He was amused at all the fuss being made over his hippy friend.

When they were ready to shoot, they gave me some instructions and began filming. First they had me hiking up the trail with my pack on my back. Then they asked me to build a fire and cook something. They filmed my cave, inside and out—my hammock, the little waterfall, the pool, my chair, and even the plastic can that doubled as a table and as a food-storage container to keep the varmints out.

"What else do you do besides cook and eat?" the director asked.

"Oh, sometimes I explore, sometimes I make things, sometimes I read," I said. "Sometimes I swim in the pool."

His face lighted up. "How about taking a little swim for us?" he asked. "That would make a good closing shot."

I hesitated and looked down. Finally, I said, "I don't have a bathing suit."

"Oh, that's no problem," he assured me. "My camera crew are professionals. They can get some good shots from far enough away that nobody can tell."

I thought for a moment. "OK," I said. "If you don't mind, I don't," and I peeled off my clothes. The crew moved back as far as they could. I climbed the boulder about twenty feet above the pool and dived in. The director and camera crew were delighted. I swam around a minute or two, the cameras whirring away. Mom stood on the side and handed me a towel as I climbed out. (It was impossible to shock her.) After I dressed, the director said he needed to ask me some questions for the interview. "Fire away!" I said.

"Your father is a multimillionaire. Your mother is in show business. You could write your own ticket—be anything you want to be. Why do you want to live in a place like this, away from the comforts of civilization?"

I thought a moment. "I guess I was a coward, running away from the discipline of life. I wanted to be able to do my own thing. Everything and everybody around me seemed so phony. It was a dog-eat-dog society. I was always getting into trouble, and I know I had a real attitude problem. Out here I feel great. I get plenty of sunshine, fresh air, and exercise climbing the mountain trails.

"I found a Bible in my cave, and it taught me about Jesus Christ. He is changing my life, and I have finally found the joy and peace I was seeking. Now that I have found Jesus, I want to tell the world. I am a free man now, for my sins are forgiven. I wish everybody could be as happy as I am, here in my cave with God, surrounded by the things He has made."

When I had finished my little speech, they filmed me playing the flute; then they put away their gear, and we all returned to Palm Springs.

"When will this be on TV?" I asked the director.

"It will be on three times today—the five o'clock news, the ten o'clock news, and the eleven o'clock news," he said.

"How can they do that?" I asked skeptically. "It's almost two o'clock now."

"Oh, you'll see," he said with a twinkle in his eye. "We're professionals, remember?" But I still had my doubts.

"There's just one thing more," I said. "Please don't say where this place is. I don't want my cave turned into a tourist attraction."

"I understand. I'll pass that on to the chief," he promised.

After we all flew down the hill, I decided to stay in town and see if they really made it in time for the five o'clock news. I had no TV at the cave, of course, and I wondered where I could go to watch. I couldn't just ring somebody's doorbell and ask if I could watch the five o'clock news. As I walked along, I spotted a hotel across the street. "That's it!" I said aloud. "I'll ask the hotel clerk if I can watch it on the TV in the lobby."

The girl at the desk reluctantly gave her permission, so I turned on the set and tuned in to the news. I was so excited, I could hardly sit still. I wished that I could have told some of my friends so they could see it, too, but it was too late for that. Just then, I saw Joe, a policeman friend, parking in front of the hotel. I ran out and grabbed him. "Come here, Joe. There's something I want to show you!" I said excitedly.

"What is it? I'm on duty, and I don't have time," he protested.

"It won't take but a few minutes," I assured him. "They're showing a local criminal on the five o'clock news."

"Oh, yeah?" His eyebrows raised. "Who's that?"

"You'll see," I said.

We had to watch a while, and Joe was about to leave, when a helicopter flying over the canyon appeared on the screen. "In Tahquitz Canyon, just a few miles out of Palm Springs, there's a veritable paradise," the newscaster began.

"Oh, no!" I groaned. "They told where my cave is!" But I didn't worry about it too much right then. I was too excited seeing myself hiking the trail, building the campfire, and cooking. I shot a glance at Joe. He sat on the edge of his chair, drinking it all in. I felt like a celebrity. I did feel apprehensive about the shot of me diving into the pool in the raw, but the camera crew handled it well, just as the director had said they would. I sighed with relief. When I made my speech at the end of the program, Joe raised his eyebrows and looked at me.

"Are you a Christian, Doug?"

No one had ever asked me that since I began reading the Bible. I wondered if I were good enough to say Yes.

"Trying to be," I responded.

"I'm glad to hear that!" Joe's eyes twinkled. "I teach a Sunday School class. Hang in there, Cave Man. You're on the right track."

Later, one of my friends told me that he watched the newscast three times that day while in jail.

I didn't know it then, but life for me would never be quite the same.

A few days later, on my way to town, I met a hiker on Cougar Trail. "Hi! Where are you headed?" I asked.

"I'm heading up to see a fellow in the third canyon. He lives in a cave—saw him on TV!" he said excitedly. With difficulty I kept a straight face.

"Really?" I asked. "Who is he? Tell me about him."

He began to tell me all about myself, adding some interesting information that even I didn't know. Finally I could stand it no longer.

"Hey, friend," I said, "there's something I'd better tell you. This guy that lives in the cave?"

"Yeah?" He looked at me questioningly.

"It's me! I'm that guy—the one you saw on TV."

He looked at me and smirked. "Very funny," he said. "You don't look anything like this guy. I'd know him anywhere!" An interesting conversation followed, and I'm not sure he ever quite believed me.

After that I never knew when I'd have visitors. Sometimes they came in singles, sometimes in groups. I would feed them banana bread and share my new-found happiness with them. I didn't need to worry about someone to witness to. My cave had been turned into a tourist attraction.

I think God had a reason for letting the TV story report the location of my cave!

13

Trying the Churches

A growing desire sprang up in my heart for fellowship with other believers, and I began to attend some of the churches in town. One place I liked to visit was called The Joshua House. It was more like a Christian home. The owner, Homer, invited people in as guests or residents. He'd conduct worship and classes to teach the street people about God. He had a work program, too, which the residents participated in. We'd sing hymns, pray, and give our testimonies. A group of pretty girls among the guests increased my interest in this place, but none of them were very interested in a grubby hippie who knew so little about being a Christian. Although I enjoyed Christian fellowship there, it really wasn't like a church. Homer attended a Pentecostal church and encouraged us to do the same.

I did visit his church, and several others too. Some of them were charismatic, and the members spoke in tongues. I attended a place called Faith Center and also studied with the Mormons and Jehovah's Witnesses. I found that most churches taught that theirs was the true church and the others were all wrong. One pastor said, "Unless you speak in tongues, you don't have the baptism of the Holy Spirit."

Back at the cave I studied up on the subject, and I learned that speaking in tongues was one of many gifts that are given to whom the *Spirit* chooses. To some He gave one gift, to others He gave other gifts, but nowhere could I find that a person had to speak in tongues to have the Holy Spirit. The fruit of the Spirit was not tongues, but love, joy, peace, etc. I also noticed that when the Holy Spirit was poured out at Pentecost, the apostles spoke real languages that were understood by the visiting Jews who spoke those languages. They didn't just praise God in some heavenly language that nobody understood.

I felt frustrated at all the disagreements Christians had among themselves, and at the way they sometimes acted so unchristian toward each other. I couldn't understand it. Didn't the Bible say, "One hope, one faith, one baptism"? Surely somewhere out there God had a true church, but which one was it? I went back to the mountains to study and pray for guidance.

One night I stood in front of my cave gazing up at the stars. The black, velvety sky glittered with pinpoints of light, and heaven seemed very real and near. "How great God is to hang all those stars in space!" Then I thought of the different churches, each claiming to be the true one. I dropped to my knees and prayed, "Lord, You've brought me a long way, and I know I still have a long way to go, but there must be a church somewhere that goes just by the Bible. I don't care which church it is. If You'll just show me, I'll accept it." I remained on my knees a moment longer. Peace filled my heart, and once again I knew that God had heard my prayer.

The next day Glen came by. Even though he didn't claim to be a Christian, he was my friend, and the frustration of my heart spilled out. "What am I going to do? One church says one thing, and another church says something else, and they all claim to believe the Bible. I read most of the Bible, but sometimes I don't understand it. I don't know which one is right." Glen didn't say much. He seemed to be going through some internal conflict.

A few days later I was lying on my hammock reading when Glen showed up again. He handed me a book.

"What's this?" I asked, looking quizzically at the cover. It had a picture of two hands holding the world. The title said, *The Great Controversy.*

"Read it," he said simply.

"But what is it?" I asked.

"Read it," he said again. He was always a man of few words. "It should answer some of your questions."

"OK, OK!" I said.

After Glen left I checked the book out more carefully. It had

678 pages, and I had never read a book even half that big in my entire life! Well, I would read a few pages to satisfy Glen. After all, there wasn't much else to do.

I skipped the introduction and started right in on chapter 1. The writer painted a picture of Jerusalem as it lay spread out at Jesus' feet. I was caught up in the story at once. Although the unfamiliar language seemed difficult to me with my limited education, I pushed on, consuming page after page.

"Wow!" I thought. "Whoever wrote this book speaks with authority." Scripture references were sprinkled generously throughout, and the narrative came alive as the words flowed.

"Who wrote this, anyway?" I asked an hour or two later. I turned to the cover and read the author's name: "Ellen G. White."

"Next to the Bible, this is the most interesting thing I've read in my life," I thought. Finally I closed the book. Lying there reading, I had grown drowsy. I drifted off to sleep, but the scenes of what I had read interlaced my dreams. When I woke up I felt impressed to read some more. For days I spent my afternoons with the book.

The next time I saw Glen, I asked, "Who's this Ellen White, anyway?"

"Well, some people believe her to be inspired."

"That's what I thought," I said. "It's obvious that God was speaking through her. I'd like to meet her and talk to her sometime."

"You're a little late." Glen smiled faintly. "She died in 1915."

"Oh." I was disappointed, but I kept reading, and finally the whole Bible began to come together and make more sense. My new book talked about the Sabbath, about when people die, and about the fight between the devil and Christ and how the church suffered during the Dark Ages.

I usually read lying on my hammock under the sycamore tree and swung back and forth by pushing my foot against a rock. It was the most relaxing place to read. There was plenty of shade, and a breeze always blew down the canyon, even when the thermometer climbed to 120. I would read a little bit, take a dive in the pool to cool off, snooze a little, and then read awhile longer. I would ponder the chapters, and often dream about what I had learned. The book absorbed all my thinking and broadened my whole impression of God and the Bible.

I thought several times that I could never finish such a big book, but every time I almost gave up I felt a voice urging me on: "Go ahead, you can do it." After several weeks I came to the final paragraph, and it thrilled my soul:

> The great controversy is ended. Sin and sinners are no more. The entire universe is clean. One pulse of harmony and gladness beats through the vast creation. From Him who created all, flow life and light and gladness, throughout the realms of illimitable space. From the minutest atom to the greatest world, all things, animate and inanimate, in their unshadowed beauty and perfect joy, declare that God is love (Ellen G. White, *The Great Controversy,* p. 678).

"Wow!" I shouted as I stood to my feet, both for the joy of having finished the long book, but more for God's ultimate triumph over Satan and sin. It was so much I could barely take it all in.

I hiked up the canyon and returned the book to Glen. "Do you have any more books like this?" I asked.

"Sure, lots of them," he said. He had been raised in a Christian home, and his parents kept sending him Christian literature, hoping to rekindle his interest. In the months that followed I read *The Desire of Ages, Steps to Christ, Patriarchs and Prophets,* and *Daniel and the Revelation.* I just feasted on the Bible and these inspiring books.

One thing bothered me, though, and that was this seventh-day Sabbath business. There was little doubt in my mind after reading the Bible and all those books that Saturday was the Sabbath, but I didn't *want* to accept it. I felt I was already different enough. I didn't want to make things worse by keeping Saturday when everyone else kept Sunday. Besides, there weren't any Christian churches that worshiped on Saturday. I decided I would find a way around it. Surely my Sunday-keeping friends had good reasons for their beliefs. I decided to ask ten ministers, but when I did I received eleven answers.

One minister said, "The law has been done away with. We don't have to keep the Sabbath."

"Oh," I said, "does that mean we don't have to keep the Ten Commandments?"

"Oh, no. We keep the other nine," he admitted.

"Do you mean the one we're supposed to forget is the one God said to remember? That doesn't make sense!"

Another minister said, "We go to church on Sunday because that's the day Jesus rose, and that's the *new* Sabbath."

"That sounds good, but I need to know where to find the Scripture for this new commandment telling us to keep the first day of the week," I replied. "If you can show me that in the Bible, I'll gladly join your church."

"Well, ah, we ah, let me put it this way." He squirmed uncomfortably. "We don't exactly have a commandment. We just have tradition."

But I didn't want tradition. Jesus said, "[Ye] reject the commandment of God, that [ye] may keep your own tradition" (Mark 7:9). I wanted Bible authority for such a change.

The next preacher was the most creative of them all. He explained it this way: "Back in the days of Joshua, when the sun stood still, and in the days of Hezekiah, when God turned the shadow back ten degrees, we lost a day, and Saturday became Sunday."

"Ah, I see. Do you mean that when Jesus was here He didn't really keep the seventh day, but the first day?" I asked.

The preacher looked confused. "Well, I'm not sure about that," he admitted.

I went back and read the story of Creation again. Suddenly I noticed something I had never seen before, and it clinched the argument for me. God blessed the seventh day *before* there was even sin in the world. That means the Sabbath was perfect, just like the world God made was perfect. Why would God change something perfect?

Furthermore, God wrote the Ten Commandments in stone, and you don't write in a stone something you plan to erase or change! I decided that a Christian is not a follower of Christians, but of Christ. Jesus worshiped on the seventh day each week and never mentioned the first day of the week, so I would just follow Jesus.

But I was still concerned. Where would I go to find people who taught all ten of the commandments?

I went to Glen and looked him in the eye. "Tell me, is there a church around where people believe these things?" I asked.

"Oh, yeah. All over the place," he answered.

"Really, what's the name of the church?"

"The Seventh-day Adventist Church," he said.

"The Seventh-day what Church? I never heard of it. The 'Seventh-day' part I can figure, but what does 'Adventist' mean?" I asked, puzzled.

"The word *advent* means the coming or arrival of something. Adventists are people who are looking forward to the second coming of Christ."

I thought to myself, "I must be an Adventist. I believe in the second coming of Christ." Aloud, I said. "How come you know so much about this stuff?"

Glen seemed a little embarrassed. "I grew up with the Bible and those books, and I attended the church ever since I was born."

"Do you mean you know all this stuff, but you don't do anything about it?" I asked in amazement. "That's incredible." I thought of all the times we smoked pot and drank together. I couldn't understand how anyone could know all about God and His marvelous love and sacrifice for man, and yet seem to ignore it.

"Let's go to church this Saturday!" I suggested enthusiastically. I had to see these wonderful people.

"Well, I don't know, Doug. I don't think I'm ready for that. You go ahead and go, and then you tell me about it."

Glen didn't seem to share my enthusiasm, because he knew what I was about to experience. In my mind I visualized a quaint little white church with a cross on the steeple. The people, of course, would be saints who were so holy, their feet barely touched the floor. They would all be smiling, carrying Bibles, and singing.

That Sabbath I arose early and put on my dirty overalls

and my hiking boots without socks. I combed my long hair, but this time I didn't tie it in a ponytail, even though it reached to my shoulders. Nor did I shave. I just smoothed the scruffy little beard that grew only on my lower chin. Bible in hand, I set off with great anticipation.

I located the street and turned my steps toward the address Glen had given me, but instead of a little country church, I found a grand, modern edifice in a prosperous neighborhood. The parking lot was filled with mostly luxury cars. I hurried inside. The red carpet felt plush under my feet. All the men wore fine suits, and the women wore expensive-looking dresses and fancy hairdos. I hadn't read anything about how Christians should dress, and suddenly I felt very out of place. Heads turned in my direction, and I'm sure they wondered if I had turned in at the wrong address. A man shook hands with me at the door and said, "I'm glad you're here." But it seemed to me that he was acting. I had been around show business all my life, and I could tell when someone was acting. Nevertheless, I went in and was directed to a seat in the back of the church.

An interesting program was in progress, and I enjoyed the mission story. When the time arrived to discuss the Sabbath School lesson, I wandered with the others down the hall to a room where chairs were arranged in a large circle. No one spoke to me, though some did give me a genuine smile. I sat down on a chair, and everyone else found seats, too, but though the room was full, the chairs on either side of me were empty.

After a few words of welcome to the class, the teacher opened his Bible and his lesson book. "The subject today is on the 490-day prophecy of Daniel 9," he began.

"Great!" I thought. I had just been reading about this in a book by Uriah Smith—*Daniel and the Revelation!* After a few preliminary remarks, he asked a question: "When did the 490-day prophecy begin?"

Suddenly I felt I was in the right place. I knew what the teacher was talking about! I nearly burst, I was so anxious to shout the answer, but I thought it might not be proper for a visitor to speak up. I glanced at the distinguished-looking people in the circle. The teacher waited, but no one spoke. They just looked at the floor and the door and the walls, but no one answered. I couldn't stand it any longer. I raised my hand.

"Yes?" the teacher said with raised eyebrows.

"Four fifty-seven B.C.," I said with a dry mouth. I hadn't been in such a large crowd in a long time.

"That's right!" the teacher replied with some surprise. "And when did the time period conclude?" he asked a few minutes later.

This time everyone looked at the hippie. Since it seemed obvious that they were all waiting for me to answer, I spoke up: "A.D. 34."

"Right again." This time the teacher didn't seem so surprised, but I couldn't understand why no one else knew the answers. Wasn't this *their* church and *their* religion? Maybe they were just being polite or modest, or maybe they were all visitors like me.

I felt a little disappointed at that first Sabbath, mostly because of the lack of warmth and fellowship. The other churches had been so friendly, had even vied for my favor. I couldn't help wondering if the attitude of the people at the Adventist church would have been the same if they had known my father was a multimillionaire. Maybe I had expected too much.

I visited the church a few more times, but I never seemed to fit in, so I kept Sabbath the best I knew on Saturday and went to church on Sunday for Christian fellowship.

I continued witnessing about my newfound faith to everyone who came by my cave, and sometimes there would be quite a gathering. Glen was impressed in spite of himself. "I don't know whether I should tell you this or not, Doug," he said one day, "but when you tell people about God, your face just lights up."

My faith increased day by day. The more I used it, the stronger it became. I often talked with a friend whose name was also Doug. He played the guitar, and I played the flute, and we would panhandle (beg for money) together on the street. My new experience as a Christian was so exciting, I just couldn't keep still about it. One day we were in town playing our instruments for money, but nobody had stopped, and nobody had given us any money, so we started talking. Soon the conversation turned to religion again.

"Well, I believe in God," Doug said, "but I don't believe in Jesus."

"I can prove that there's a Jesus," I said confidently.

"And how are you going to do that?" he asked skeptically.

"How much money do we need right now?" I asked.

"Well, it would be nice if we got a couple of dollars apiece. Then we could go eat out," he said.

"All right," I said, "I'm going to pray right now to Jesus, and we're going to get four dollars." So I bowed my head, and I said, "Lord, help us to get four dollars so we can buy a good meal, and help Doug to know that You are real. I ask in Jesus' name, amen."

We began to play again, and soon a lady walking by stopped to listen. When we were through, I asked her if she had any spare change.

"Well," she thought quietly for a moment, "normally I don't do this sort of thing, but today is my son's birthday, and he's just about your age." She dug into her purse and pulled out some money. "Will four dollars help?" she asked. I assured her that it would. As she walked away she must have wondered why my friend was staring in blank shock with his mouth open.

Before long, he, too, had accepted Jesus Christ as his Saviour.

14

If at First You Don't Succeed

The first time I saw Karyn, we were both only fifteen. She and a bunch of girls had just left a party and were standing on the street corner, laughing, talking loudly, and acting silly. I thought, "What a bunch of dingbats. Cute, but silly."

She wasn't very interested in the likes of me, either. She preferred dating older boys with cars.

I saw her occasionally around town after that and remembered who she was, but so many other things were going on in my life. However, about two years later, when I was just starting to read the Bible, our paths crossed again. My friend Rico and I had gone to the pool hall to goof off and play a little pool, and I saw Karyn with another girl at a table across the room. It turned out that the other girl was Rico's girl, so they introduced Karyn and me, and then went to the bar, leaving the two of us together. It was an awkward situation. Neither of us had planned it that way.

"Do you want to shoot a game?" I asked.

"Not really," she said.

"OK. Let's go somewhere else, then," I suggested. I held the door open, and we went out and ambled along, just talking. When we came to a liquor store, against my better judgment I went in and bought a bottle of wine. "Let's go to the park and find a cool place to sit," I said. "I bought us a little refreshment."

"No, thanks, Doug. I don't drink anymore," she answered.

"What do you mean, you don't drink?" I asked, disbelieving. "Everybody drinks!" But she stood her ground.

"And I suppose you read the Bible too?" I asked, half sarcastically.

She stopped and looked at me in surprise. "As a matter of fact, I do. How did you know?"

"I don't know. Just by putting two and two together, I guess. That's funny," I went on. "I've been reading the Bible too." We walked a long time in the cool desert night, talking about the Bible and religion. The more we talked, the more we found to talk about.

We saw each other a lot after that, and a few weeks later we were married. We moved into town, but we didn't like city life, so one day we put our belongings on our backs and started hitchhiking north up the California coast. We didn't really know where we were going, so we took our time. Sometimes we would fall asleep by a freeway on-ramp, only to be awakened by the sprinklers at five o'clock in the morning. Once we walked off the road near Big Sur, California, and went to sleep in the woods. When we woke up, a park ranger was standing over us. "I don't mind your camping here," he said, "but you might want to know that you're lying in poison oak." The remainder of that week was very uncomfortable!

In Ukiah, California, a young couple stopped to give us a ride. "Where ya headed?" the driver asked.

"We don't know for sure," I said. "We're praying that God will show us. Where are you all going?"

A little surprised, the driver said, "You don't want to go where we live. It's out in the middle of nowhere—a little town called Covelo. It's surrounded by national forest."

"Hmmm. Are there any caves up there?"

"Well, I suppose," the young man said.

"Are there any churches?" Karyn asked.

"That's all there are," the wife replied. "There isn't even a theater in town."

Karyn and I felt impressed to go to Covelo, and we quickly fell in love with the beauty of the pine-covered mountains. We lived in a cave in the national forest for a while, and we looked around for land. Soon we found a place that we really wanted. The only problem was money. The only work I could find was seasonal. At summer's end we were forced to return to Palm

Springs so I could support our growing family, for soon we would be parents.

I tried odd jobs for a while, but nothing really good came along. Finally I found work selling and delivering meat. I could see immediately that I was part of a three-party arrangement. Why not eliminate the middleman and make the profit myself?

Dad helped me to buy a nice little used VW. I had never owned a car before, and knew next to nothing about their upkeep. I thought the oil went in the radiator, but the VW didn't *have* a radiator. I learned fast!

I had a sign painted on the side, Doug Batchelor's Whole- sale Prime Beef Steaks. After printing business cards and making some contacts, I put a cooler in the back of the little VW. I bought a section of beef, and a friend showed me how to cut it into steaks. I soon had a prosperous business going, selling steaks wholesale. Business was good right from the start.

I learned some interesting things during my brief beef ven- ture. One day a customer asked me if I could get her some prime pork. I knew about the grades of beef: prime, choice, good, and fair. I had seen graded chicken, but I'd have to do some checking on the pork.

I went to one of my butcher friends. When he heard my question, he laughed. "The Department of Agriculture doesn't think you should feed that stuff to your dogs. They're not going to grade it. That stuffs swarming with 'bugs.' They even print pamphlets telling you to make sure you cook it thoroughly to kill all the trichina larvae."

"Yuck!" That revolted me. Then I remembered reading something in the Bible about swine's flesh. Some preachers told me those laws had been done away with, but that didn't make sense. Didn't the human body still respond to the food put into it, the same as it did during the time of the children of Israel? Wasn't it still subject to disease germs and parasites?

I learned something else from experience too. Since I sold prime beef, I decided I should use my own products. Soon I was eating New York steak for breakfast, T-bone steak for lunch, and fillet mignon for dinner. But then I noticed that I felt run-down all the time, with no energy. My behavior began to change too. At night I would sit and watch TV and eat a quart of ice cream by myself—yes, a whole quart! I felt my spiritual life being numbed, and I had less inclination to resist temptation. My cave-man diet of rice, beans, bread, and fruit had given me a feeling of strength and vigor. For the first time I realized what an impact diet had on my physical, spiritual, and moral well-being. I was making good money in the meat business, but somehow Karyn and I were never able to save. The more we made, the more we spent.

"Let's give Covelo another try," I said one day. "I think we can make it this time." We traded in our VW for an old broken-down Ford pickup. After nursing it for 700 miles, we arrived in Covelo, and we soon found 160 acres of beautiful, undeveloped land that we were able to buy on terms that we could handle. We lived in a tent while we built a small house on the property out of scrap lumber. It wasn't a mansion, but it was ours, and we loved it! I started a small firewood business.

We began attending the Presbyterian church, but I couldn't forget about the Sabbath and other things I had learned. There was a Seventh-day Adventist church right across the street from the Presbyterian church, and I wondered if this congregation might be friendlier. I had met a fellow named Duane who liked church and religion, so one Saturday he and I decided to visit the Adventist church. Karyn chose to stay at home with Rachel, our new baby girl.

My feelings that morning were a mixture of anticipation and dread. "What if they aren't friendly? What if they don't like the way I look? Well, no matter. It's the Sabbath, and I have as much right to be there as they do!" I guess I had a chip on my shoulder that morning as I dressed, because I dug out my old overalls and found a scroungy-looking shirt and put them on. I tied my hair back in a ponytail.

I got on my motorcycle and roared off to pick up Duane. In those days it was considered "cool" to wear tattered old blue jeans, and he really looked "cool." One of the back pockets of his jeans had been torn off, and his bare skin revealed the fact that he wasn't even wearing underwear! I almost felt embarrassed for him, but I didn't mention it.

A smiling man waited for us at the door and gave us a firm handshake. He welcomed us warmly and invited us inside, where a sweet little old lady shook our hands and asked us to sign the guest book. We went into the church and sat down. People were still arriving, and we watched them as they came in. I saw a lot of gray hair and bald heads that day. A couple came in and walked to the pew ahead of us, but before they sat down they both turned around, introduced themselves, and shook hands.

The sermon that day seemed to burst spontaneously from the old pastor's heart. He had a warmth and sincerity about him that touched me. I drank in the words of life like a thirsty man in a dry desert. After church, people crowded about us, welcoming us, and inviting us home to dinner. No one even seemed to notice our clothes, and I felt a little ashamed by now. Duane and I were so overwhelmed with all the invitations and attention that we hardly knew what to do. Finally the old pastor, Joe Phillips, and his wife prevailed over the others, and we went home with them. I'm sure these kind people never dreamed that someday this hippie would be their pastor!

We sat down to a wholesome meal of simply prepared food—a vegetarian loaf, potatoes, two or three vegetables, homemade whole-wheat bread, a tossed salad, and apple pie! "Help yourselves," Pastor Joe invited. "My wife's the best cook in town, and you'll hurt her feelings if you don't eat!" Duane and I didn't hurt their feelings that day. We just about emptied every bowl on the table. Our host and hostess were both amazed and pleased.

After lunch, Pastor Joe said, "Why don't we all go into the living room and have a Bible study?" I welcomed the idea, and soon had my Bible open, discussing the Scriptures with Pastor and Mrs. Phillips. Duane fell asleep in his chair.

The next Sabbath Karyn attended church with me, and after that we attended church every Sabbath, and the pastor and his wife had us home for lunch. We always studied the Bible in the afternoon. However, the pastor would hardly get into the subject when I would realize it was something I had already learned on my own. When we studied Daniel and Revelation, I knew all the hoofs and the horns and their dates as well. One day Pastor Joe said, "Doug, you're almost ready for baptism."

"What do you mean, Pastor—almost? I'm ready now," I said. "I believe everything this church teaches."

He hesitated. "How about the smoking, Doug? Are you ready to give that up?"

It was my turn to hesitate. "Well, now, I don't know about that. I don't see what that has to do with my love for God. I've given up all my really *bad* vices, like smoking pot and drinking and drugs and stealing and lying. But smoking isn't that bad. I only smoke about half a pack a day, you know. Anyhow, I know the Lord loves me and answers my prayers."

"That's right, Doug, He does love you," Pastor Joe said patiently. "And He's teaching you, and leading you along step by step. But as long as you're addicted to cigarettes, you're chained to the devil. Can you imagine Jesus blowing smoke in someone's face while He's talking to them about the love of His Father?"

I knew Jesus was our example, and the thought of Him smoking a cigarette seemed so ridiculous that I laughed.

"You see," the pastor continued, "when you're baptized, it represents a new birth, and the Lord doesn't want His babies to smoke. Would you, Doug?"

"Well, when you put it that way, no," I admitted.

I began thinking about the struggle to give up drinking. I had argued with the Lord. "But Lord, I like drinking. It's fun."

And the Lord said, "Go ahead and drink, Doug." I don't mean that the Lord was pleased with my drinking. He just meant that He wouldn't force me to stop. Little by little I began to see all the heartache my drinking caused. I'd wake up in jail or be sick all day and throw up, or I'd wake up and find out I'd made a fool of myself and embarrassed someone I cared about. Once I found out I had wrecked a car that didn't even belong to me. I heard the Lord saying, "Doug, are you enjoying yourself?" It finally dawned on me that God only wants Christians to give up what's harmful to them, either physically or spiritually. When I finally figured it out, I gave up drinking. But I knew right away that smoking would be harder.

Karyn kicked the habit relatively easily. The doctor explained to her that our baby was born premature because she smoked. "Smoking doesn't just harm you," he said. "It harms your baby too."

One day, when she came into the room, Karyn noticed the cigarette she had left lying on the edge of the ashtray. The smoke was drifting right over to where little Rachel lay sleeping. "What am I doing!" Karyn exclaimed. "It's bad enough that I'm destroying my own lungs. How can I destroy my baby's lungs too?" That day when I came in, she said, "Doug, I'm going to see how long I can go without smoking." And that was it. She never smoked again.

Karyn was baptized without me.

For some people it's easy, but for others the cigarette demon kicks and screams before he lets go. I wrestled with myself, trying to muster up enough courage to make the break. One day I said, "Tomorrow I'll quit," and I threw my cigarettes away and tried to forget about them. But the next day I wanted a cigarette so badly that my hands shook. I hurried to the store and got some more. "That was sure a waste of money," I told myself. I smoked half the pack within the next few hours, but my conscience haunted me the whole time. "OK, OK, so I'll try again."

And so the battle raged for months.

I loved the Adventist Church because it stood for something. I knew I could have joined any number of churches without giving up smoking or drinking, but I knew if I wanted to join the Adventist Church I'd have to take up my cross and follow Him. One of Pastor Joe's favorite sayings became mine: "If you don't stand for something, you'll fall for anything." I wanted desperately to join, but I didn't—not then.

A few weeks later, as I drove my aging truck along the road, I heard a pop, followed by a hiss, and then a flap-flap-flap sound. "Oh, no! Not another!" I sighed. It was the second flat tire that day. My truck was croaking before my very eyes. Within the last twenty-four hours, a headlight fell out, the tailgate fell off, and the engine started smoking.

As I jacked up the wheel and removed the tire, I thought of those new Datsun four-wheel-drive pickups I had seen advertised. How I wanted one! I began to daydream. If I had the money, I'd get one with a king cab for my growing family—one with a five-speed transmission, a winch in front, and a flatbed, so I could carry wood.

I tightened the last nut, snapped the hubcap back on, and started the engine, but my mind was still on those new Datsun trucks. Finally I blurted out, "Lord, I'd even give up smoking if You'd give me a truck like that!"

I never claimed that I heard God's voice speak to me audibly, though I have heard it many times speak to my conscience, but suddenly I heard a voice echoing in the cab of that old pickup: "You'd quit smoking for a truck, but you wouldn't quit smoking for Me?"

I was shocked, and I sat several minutes listening for another voice. Then I thought, "Jesus died on the cross for me, and He only asked me to give up things that hurt me, yet I won't quit smoking for Him." I had to have a truck. "Oh, Lord, please forgive me!" I cried. "I didn't mean that, and with Your help, I'll never smoke again!"

When I got home, I took my cigarettes and threw them down the outhouse because I knew I wouldn't go after them there, and by the grace of God, I've never smoked another one. Two weeks later I was baptized.

Exactly ten years down the road the Lord gave me a Datsun 4x4 with a winch, king cab, and five-speed. I hadn't even prayed for power windows and cruise control! But I wondered, "Lord, why did You wait ten years?"

He told me that during that time, I had saved enough money from not smoking to buy it.

15

But Lord, I Could Never Be a Preacher!

ver since I accepted Jesus in the cave, I had talked to people about God's love. I turned almost every conversation into religion and what God had done for me. I talked to the man at the garage, to hippies, street people, hitchhikers, our neighbors—everybody.

When the pastor announced in church, shortly after my baptism, that an evangelistic series would begin in two weeks, I thought of all those people I had been talking to, and many of them seemed to long for the peace and happiness that I felt. I decided that I would invite them to the meetings.

The evening the meetings began, our small church overflowed. I stood at the door and watched for the friends I had invited. Many of my neighbors in the mountains attended that first night and continued to come night after night. When we had our first baptism, ten of the twelve who were baptized were those I had studied with and invited. "What a joy to serve God!" I thought. "This is happiness, and it doesn't leave a hangover."

One day Pastor Joe approached me. "Why don't you preach for us, Doug? Your love for God and your enthusiasm reach people's hearts, and you need to share it from the pulpit."

Suddenly I felt timid. Me, preach? "Oh no, Pastor! You have the wrong guy. I could never be a preacher! I don't have the education, and I wouldn't know what to say. No thanks, Pastor, I just couldn't do it."

"You don't have to have a college education," he persisted. "Just get up and tell the people what God has done for you. That's all you have to do."

"Oh, I don't think I could," I said emphatically.

The pastor dropped the subject for then, but he had planted an idea in my mind, and the Holy Spirit watered it. When he brought up the subject again, I resisted a little less, and finally I agreed to try.

If I live to be a hundred, I will never forget that first "sermon" I preached! I didn't even own a suit, and I forgot to put on a tie, but it wasn't my clothes that bothered me. I sat nervously on the platform waiting for the moment of truth. My hands perspired, and I could feel my heart thumping in my throat. When I finally got up to speak, I laid my Bible in front of me and grasped the edges of the pulpit. I was glad to have something to hide behind so the audience couldn't see my knees knocking together. When I opened my mouth to speak, the voice that came out didn't sound like mine. I kept swallowing and smacking my lips because my mouth was so dry. But those dear people! Bless their hearts, they gave me their undivided attention. Pastor and Mrs. Phillips sat on the front row, and every time I made some point they nodded and said "Amen." The people's response to my feeble words gave me encouragement to go on, and somehow I got through. When I shook hands at the door that day, many had tears in their eyes as they told me what a blessing my sermon had been to them.

"Me? A blessing?" I thought. I noticed that several of the saints who complimented the sermon wore hearing aids. I figured that they must have been broken that morning.

I spoke rather frequently after that, and each time it seemed a little easier.

"Doug, you really should go to college and train for the ministry," Pastor Phillips urged. "The Lord has given you a special talent for this work, and I know how much you love sharing the gospel. His work needs you."

I studied that kindly old gentleman's face. To myself I thought, "If I ever do become a preacher, I want to be just like you." What an inspiration he was to me! To him I said, "Sure, Pastor Joe, we'll pray about it."

In the end I *did* go to school to take a few classes. Dear old Dad! He had always wanted me to get an education, even if it was a religious one, so he was happy to help, and for six months

But Lord, I Could Never Be a Preacher!

I attended Southwestern Adventist College in Keene, Texas. It was one of the best things I ever did. I had goofed off so much as a teenager in school that I had convinced myself I wasn't very bright, but at Southwestern I made straight A's. Now I knew I could learn something if I wanted to.

I checked a book out of the library—*The Autobiography of Benjamin Franklin.* I was amazed as I read how this man dropped out of school and ran away from home, yet he learned to speak and write in seven languages! He invented bifocal glasses, the Franklin stove, the postal system, public libraries, and fire departments. He made electrical discoveries, started newspapers and magazines, and was the first United States ambassador to France. And he was a vegetarian!

I thought, "If he could teach himself, so can I. Jesus promised that 'I can do all things through Christ.'" Since becoming a Christian I had learned many things I never dreamed I could do, including playing the flute, guitar, harmonica, piano, and trumpet. I had learned to speak a little Spanish and how to fly a plane and windsurf, and at the time was learning to sing—though my friends were begging me to give that up!

After college, I worked with Pastor Marvin Moore in Texas. He was a tall, friendly fellow who looked like Abraham Lincoln. We did some Revelation Seminars together and made a good team, for the Lord really blessed our efforts, and many were baptized. Later that year I was invited to join the famous gospel singing group called Heritage Singers—as their devotional speaker. I'm still working on the singing!

God knew what He was doing, for as I stood before the audience night after night part way through each Heritage Singers concert, telling the people what God had done for me and inviting them to follow Jesus, the last vestiges of stage fright dropped away. Eighteen months of speaking five times a week more than made up for what I had missed in the way of formal education.

16

Indian Tales

O ne day while I was at the Heritage Singers' office, the telephone rang. "This is Leroy Moore," a voice said. "I'm in charge of Seventh-day Adventist Native American work in North America. I have heard of your success in evangelism. How would you like to come to La Vida Mission and work for the Navajos?"

I thought of my days among the Indians when I lived with my uncle in New Mexico. I had really liked the people. Still, there were some things I wanted to forget.

"I'm sorry, Mr. Moore," I said. "We have our trailer loaded and will be leaving shortly for California. I'm working with the Heritage Singers."

"I see." He paused. "Well, since you'll be passing through New Mexico anyway, why don't you stop by La Vida Mission and at least look us over? We can put you up for the night."

"Thanks, Mr. Moore," I said. "We'll stop by, and I'll make your offer a matter of prayer. I'll be in touch."

In my heart I had already decided we weren't interested, but God had other plans. Even before we pulled into the mission, our trailer developed a funny sway and made an unusual noise. "It's a good thing we're almost there," I told Karyn. "Something's wrong with the trailer."

We arrived at the mission a few minutes later, and as we pulled into the yard, the trailer wheel fell off. Of all the places we could have broken down on this whole 2,000-mile trip, we broke down in the mission yard!

"You need a new set of wheel bearings," one of the men

there told me. He had taken off a wheel and showed me the worn parts.

"How long will that take?" I asked.

"A little while, I would guess," the man replied. "These one-horse garages don't carry much. They'll probably have to order from Albuquerque. I'd say two days, at least."

I sighed. "Well, that should give us a chance to look things over." When Karyn and I saw the needs of the Navajo people, we knew that this was where God wanted us.

"We'll stay," I told Leroy a little later.

The mission had purchased an old house in Waterflow, New Mexico, that was to be our home. They wanted us to raise up a church there, but the people occupying the house hadn't moved out yet, nor even finished packing, for that matter. They left old furniture, unwanted junk, and garbage. They even left their dirty breakfast dishes on the table. In about a month we got it painted and cleaned up, and it wasn't bad. At least it was spacious.

Nearby stood a mobile home owned by the mission, but rented out to an Indian family. The yard was littered with telltale beer cans. Hardly a tree could be seen in the surrounding country just hard desert floor and the flat-topped mesas that stood like silent sentinels of a desolate land.

The work began small. We started by converting an old hamburger stand into a meeting place, and we held a Revelation Seminar in a tent. The Lord blessed our efforts, and the work grew. Soon over a hundred people were crowding into that small building.

The mission was only seventy miles from my uncle's trading post, and I often thought of him and his family and some of my other friends. One day a broken-down pickup came hobbling into the yard where I was working. The vehicle wasn't so old, just in bad shape. The doors were dented, one was strapped shut, the windshield had a crack, and the tires were bald. An Indian man opened the door and slowly stumbled out. He had long, stringy hair; a shiny, scarred face; hollow eyes; and a potbelly. I guessed him to be a man in his fifties. He limped over to me and looked around cautiously.

"Do you know a guy named Doug Batchelor?" he asked.

I was surprised to hear my name. I looked intently at the

man, but found no clues as to his identity. "Well, yes, I'm Doug Batchelor," I said, still puzzled.

He hesitated an instant, looked at me intently, and then his face lit up. "Doug! Doug!" he cried. "Remember me? It's Ken!" He staggered over to me and embraced me with a great big bear-hug. I hugged him back, still not sure who this guy was.

"Ken?" I asked.

"Yeah! Ken Platero. Remember? We used to ride motorcycles together when you lived with your uncle."

Suddenly it dawned on me. This was my drinking buddy, the one I had talked into taking me to the bar. The one who said, "Drinking is trouble."

"It *is* you! I didn't recognize you!" I said. "It's been a long time—ten years, about."

"Something like that. I heard from your uncle that you were here. He tells me that you're a Christian now. Is that true?"

"That's right, Ken. I'm a Seventh-day Adventist."

"I'm so glad." He seemed to speak from the depths of his soul. "I need God in my life. I've got nothing but trouble!" Worry wrinkles creased his brow, and when he sighed, I could tell that his sorrow lay deep.

"What kind of trouble?" I asked.

"My wife is leaving me. I'm in trouble with the law, and my life's a mess." He seemed so sad. "I need the Lord."

"I understand how you feel," I said. "I'm the chief of sinners. Let's pray about it." Ken and I knelt in the yard, and I prayed for him and his family. Tears streamed down his face as we rose from our knees. He took my hand in both of his. "I'm going to come to your church. I want you to keep praying for me and my family."

"I'll be looking for you, Ken. And you'll always be in my prayers," I assured him.

"You've been the best friend I've ever had," he said as he climbed into his truck.

As he drove off I thought, "No, Ken. I've been your worst enemy. I got you started down the wrong road. 0 God, what have I done?" I cried. "Have I destroyed a man's life by my bad example when I was young and foolish?"

I never saw Ken again. I hoped he'd make it to some of our

meetings, but he never did. I tried to find out where he lived, but couldn't. Maybe I didn't try hard enough. The memory was so painful. "Lord," I prayed, "if there is anything I can do to redeem this great wickedness, please show me what it is!"

Even while I prayed, I stood in front of the mobile home that stood next to my house. Who were the people who lived there? Karyn and I knew that they had three children, and that they were intelligent, good-looking people. Later we learned that their names were Tom and Alaice Begay. She had a good job as a computer operator, along with office skills. He had been to Vietnam, spoke both Navajo and English fluently, and was a highly skilled electrician. But the day I stood in the yard and prayed, they were the mystery people.

We had reached out to them and tried to be good neighbors. Karyn had made bread and other goodies and taken them to the door. Alaice would open the door a crack and smile and accept them politely, and then close the door. We always waved and spoke when we saw them, but they remained aloof. We wondered what the problem was.

Then one night we heard a frantic knock at the door. The doorbell rang, and the knocking came again before I could reach the door. I quickly opened it, and there stood eleven-year-old Tracy, the oldest of the three neighbor children. Her eyes were wide with terror. "Come quick!" she pleaded. "My father is killing my mother!"

I hesitated for a split second as my mind raced. For an instant I thought that I probably should call the police and keep out of my neighbor's business, but if I did that, I might never reach them with the gospel. I bolted out the door and ran across the yard to their door and began knocking loudly. Inside I could hear thumping and screaming and scuffling. I soon realized that no one was going to open the door, so I jerked it open and rushed in.

There the man stood in the bedroom, leaning against one wall, panting and out of breath, glaring at his wife. She sat on the floor, holding her bleeding nose and mouth, sobbing and groaning. Her brown cheek was bruised and swollen. He barely glanced in my direction when I entered the room. He kept his eyes fixed on her, yelling and cursing, some in English, some in

Navajo. He threw a punch at her, but missed. She screamed and cowered before him. He swung again and missed. I realized that he was only trying to intimidate her, not hit her. The smell of alcohol in the room was powerful.

I couldn't just stand there and watch, so I stepped between them and helped her to her feet.

"Oh, you got the preacher to come and rescue you, huh?" he snarled.

"Stop it," I said, "let her alone!"

"Oh, yeah, who invited you here?" he growled. "Get out!"

I stood my ground. "I'm just trying to help," I said calmly. "I could have called the police, but I didn't. This is no way to settle problems. If you hate her that much, leave, but don't beat her up."

"It's her fault!" he yelled. Then they began yelling accusations at each other, and he began swinging at her again.

I'm only five-nine, and Tom was six-one, but I grabbed him in a full Nelson, with my arms under his armpits and my fingers laced tightly at the back of his neck. When she saw he could not get away, she attacked him and began pulling his hair.

"Cut it out!" I yelled. I threw him against one wall and her against the other—it wasn't that hard since they were both half-drunk—and stepped between them. Our chests heaved as we stood there. The two younger children cowered in a corner, crying softly.

As our heart rates slowed and we began to breathe normally once more, I said, "Why don't we sit down and talk this out like rational human beings?"

They stumbled into the living room and sat down. They were both dressed up—or had been, apparently—to go to a party. They wouldn't talk much, but I made up my mind not to leave until one of them left. In a few minutes Alaice got up and went out, with the children behind her.

That blew the lid off their secret. Karyn and I soon learned that this was the most notorious family in these parts. They had been in the headlines for years. Tom was tall, handsome, and macho. Alaice was attractive and flirtatious, and they both drank. They were jealous of each other, and when they drank, the fights erupted.

I debated what to do. Should I report them to the mission and have them evicted? If I did that, I would lose all hope of ever winning them for Christ. What would Jesus do? I decided that He would be their friend. "Well, Lord, I'll try," I thought to myself.

When Tom got in trouble for pulling a gun on a man who had insulted him, I went to court with him. When he got in jail, I helped him get out.

Karyn befriended Alaice and the kids. She made cookies for them and had them all over for a little party. Sometimes when there was trouble, Alaice and the kids, or sometimes just the kids, would watch from the safety of our house. Two or three police cars would arrive in their yard, red-and-blue lights flashing, while the officers got out and went in to referee the fights.

One night when I was gone for a few days holding an evangelistic series, Karyn sat in her bed reading. Suddenly the back bedroom door opened, and Alaice came charging in. She looked at Karyn and said, "I'm sorry!" and went running on through. Seconds later, Tom came chasing after her with a broom. Karyn didn't even get out of bed. We had become accustomed to this behavior. The whole world seemed an uglier place because of their drinking and brawling.

Tom would stay sober for a few weeks and get a job, making good money. Then he would go on a drinking spree. And not only did he spend all his money, he would also do destructive things. Once he wrecked his new car. Another time he threw something at their large, expensive TV and cracked it.

Often when Tom was sober I would go over and talk to him about the love of God. At first he had his guard up, but I just kept being friendly and kept visiting. He knew we cared, and he began to listen. He had an interest in spiritual matters. He had read some Christian books and had even gone to church. Some Baptist friends had taught him a few things about being a Christian, but he needed to learn what it means to follow Jesus, how important it is to study the Bible and have a private devotional life, how we need to teach our children and pray with them. These were new concepts to him.

We planned another Revelation Seminar, and I really hoped I could get Tom and his family to come. I talked to him one day. "Tom," I said, "you owe me one."

"What do you mean?"

"I've gone to court with you, I've stood by your side, I've fended off the police, and I've been a good neighbor. Now I want a favor from you."

"All right, Doug, what do you want?" he asked.

"I want you to come to these meetings that I'm starting," I said. "We're going to be studying the book of Revelation, and you'll enjoy them."

"Oh, no, Doug. I can't do that."

"And why not?" I countered. "Why don't you just come the first couple of nights? Then if you don't like them, you can quit."

"OK, I'll come," he said.

"That's a promise?" I asked.

"It's a promise."

I knew I had to get him while he was sober.

The other churches were not encouraging. "You can't get anywhere with the Navajos," they warned. "You'll be lucky if you get fifty to come out to a meeting. It'll more likely be ten or fifteen."

"Let's set our goal for a hundred," I told my little church. "The Lord's arm is not shortened. He can bless us." So we prayed for a hundred.

On opening night we had 375, counting the children! The gymnasium was packed. "It's the most spectacular thing I've ever seen among the American Indians," Leroy Moore told us. "It's incredible how, all of a sudden, these people want to hear the gospel!"

The greatest thrill of the whole evening was when Tom and Alaice arrived with their three children. The people were pouring in, and our poor staff was just swamped trying to get everyone registered.

"May I help?" Alaice asked Karyn, who was working furiously.

"You surely may!" Karyn said gratefully as she set up a spot for Alaice at the table.

As the meetings proceeded, it was interesting to see the change taking place in this family. Alaice began to smile. Then the children began smiling. Tom and Alaice, and even Tracy, the oldest of their children, participated and contributed when we discussed the questions and answers.

They sat at the front table, and I watched them studying, thinking, and writing down answers. When we had discussions, they raised their hands, and sometimes they just called out answers.

We held the meetings six nights a week for six weeks. One night Tom was not in his place when I began to preach. My heart felt heavy, and I cried out inwardly, "0 Lord, don't let him be drinking!" When he came in a few minutes later and sat with his family, I sighed with relief.

I began to notice changes in their home-life too. One day I looked out the window. Tom and Alaice were picking up the beer cans and putting them in plastic bags. Then they raked and cleaned the yard. A few days later Karyn and I looked out and saw the whole family gathered outside digging up the ground to make a garden. Tom and Alaice were spraying each other with the garden hose. The kids ran toward their father and shouted, "Spray us too!" Tom turned the hose on them, and soon everybody was wet, and laughter filled the air.

What a contrast! Before the Revelation Seminar began, I had never seen the children smile in the presence of their parents, much less laugh. In fact, they wouldn't even play in their own yard. They came to our house to play.

One Sabbath they surprised us by coming to Sabbath School and church. What a striking family they were, tastefully dressed, every one of them good looking, from Tom and Alaice right down to the youngest child.

At the conclusion of the Revelation Seminar almost 100 people indicated that they believed and wanted to be baptized. We had been warned not to be hasty in baptizing the Navajos. "They are such a gentle people and wish to please," Leroy told us. "Be sure they are being baptized because they are convicted by the Holy Spirit, not just trying to please someone."

So we carefully visited each one before we had a baptism, and this, of course, took some time. During the waiting time, we continued holding church services, and Tom and Alaice attended faithfully Sabbath by Sabbath. One day my interpreter didn't show up. What could I do? I didn't speak much Navajo, and many of the older Navajos didn't speak English.

"I'll translate," Tom volunteered, and he did. It brought tears to my eyes, watching those people leaning forward in their seats so they wouldn't miss a word and seeing Tom's face all aglow as he stood before the class. He didn't just translate. He taught that class. I don't know who was happier, Tom or I. Tom and Alaice were baptized a few months later, and it seemed that the whole world was a better place because of what the gospel did for that one family!

17

Going Home

The screen door banged behind me as I hurried into the house. "Who wants to go to Covelo?" I called out. The kids came running, and Karyn put the last pan of bread into the oven and turned to me with dancing eyes.

"We do, we do!" the children chorused.

"How come we're going to Covelo?" Karyn asked.

"I got a phone call from Dave, and I need to get home and take care of some business at our cabin there. How soon can you pack up a few things?"

"We can't go until the bread's done," Karyn said, "but I can get packed right now."

"That's too soon," I said. "Actually, we aren't leaving until in the morning, but we'll get an early start."

The next morning everybody popped out of bed as soon as they were called, and we were on our way by daylight.

"Will we get to see Pastor Joe and Mrs. Phillips?" Micah asked as we pulled out onto the highway. The Phillipses were like grandparents to our kids, and they loved them dearly.

"Sure will," I assured him. "We'll see all our church family!"

Happy chatter filled the car as we all savored the anticipation of homecoming. But by midafternoon the talk died down, and everyone began dropping off to sleep. I was left alone with my thoughts as the car ate up the miles.

The Phillipses. What good memories flooded my mind, and how they had helped our family and shaped our lives! "It must be the practical way they live their religion," I thought. My mind played back a scene from early in our acquaintance.

111

"What am I going to do?" I asked Karyn one day. "We've got to have a chain saw if I'm going to sell firewood. That's the only way I can make enough to make payments on the land, and the bank turned me down flat."

"Why? What did they say?" she asked.

"They said they couldn't loan me money because I didn't have credit." If I hadn't been a grown man, I would have cried. Was I going to lose my land before I could make the first payment?

"But how are you going to get credit if you can't borrow any money?" She looked at me with worried eyes.

"That's what I asked *them!*" I said. "For all the good it did. They weren't about to take a chance on the likes of me. I'm just a grubby hippie to them."

But when Pastor Joe heard of my plight, he didn't hesitate. He reached right into his pocket, pulled out his checkbook, and began to write.

"Pay me back when you can," he said, smiling as he held out a check for $300. My mouth dropped open. This man scarcely knew me! I resolved that paying him back would be one of my first priorities, and it was!

Pastor Phillips had "retired" and moved to Covelo before I was born. There he built a church and later a school. Some ministers look upon the ministry as a career with a good retirement, but not Pastor Joe. He refused to retire. He was going to work for the Lord until he dropped.

I couldn't help being impressed with his lifestyle. In his eighties he returned to Covelo and built his own house—with some help, of course—but there he was with the best of them, carrying lumber and working like a man in his fifties.

"There must be something to this vegetarian lifestyle," I remembered telling Karyn one day. I thought of the wonderful vegetables they grew. They practically lived out of their garden, for two reasons. First, for their health, but of no less importance to them was the money they saved. The less they spent on food, the more they had to give to spread the gospel. Out of their small monthly income they gave more than 50 percent to various ministries and projects!

I knew that the prayers of this dedicated man had done as

much as anything to help me make my decision for Christ. Joe and Miriam Phillips had a list of more than fifty people that Joe prayed for every morning. Pastor Joe mentioned each person by name and prayed about his or her problems and welfare, and he spent a *lot* of time with his Bible. I'm sure that was the secret to his spiritual power. He never seemed to have a trace of impatience or a temper, but under the most stressful situations always maintained a gentle, kind composure.

And Mrs. Phillips. What a powerful witness her life was! She always worked alongside her husband and even helped build the house. I remembered the time he was carrying a long piece of lumber and swung around and whacked her a good one. "Joe!" she said.

"Oh, sorry, dear," he answered, and they both went on about their business. I chuckled aloud at the memory of it.

"What are you laughing about?" Karyn wanted to know, rousing from her nap.

"Oh, I was just thinking of the Phillipses," I said.

"They are a precious couple, aren't they?" she said.

"Since Mrs. Phillips has been married to Pastor Joe, I know her guardian angel has had to work overtime. Remember the time he nearly backed the car over her?" I asked.

"I remember!" she said. "They remind me of some of the Laurel and Hardy movies I used to watch when I was a kid."

"Yeah, that's a good comparison. Remember the time we saw a car coming down the wrong way on the freeway, and it turned out to be the Phillipses?"

"Do I! That was scary," Karyn laughed. "It seems funny now, but they could have been killed. They're such a cute couple. She must be a head taller than he, and when she laughs her mouth reaches ear to ear."

I grinned at the thought. "Mrs. Phillips is the only one I ever saw who will stand up in the middle of the sermon and interrupt the preacher."

"But she's never rude." Karyn hastened to her defense. "I like the way she closes her eyes and quotes Scripture without a mistake."

"Yes," I agreed. "Her face just shines. I always feel like we've had a message straight from heaven."

"I think everyone thinks so. They all stop and listen, and give her their undivided attention," Karyn said. "Anyhow, Pastor Joe seems to appreciate it."

The trip to California was hard. We drove straight through, hardly stopping at all, and we were certainly glad to see our mountain home still standing as we pulled up in the yard. We climbed out stiffly. "Everybody carry something in," I reminded them as the kids made a dash for the door.

The time in Covelo passed too quickly. There was so much to do and so little time to do it. We did take time out for a good visit with the Phillipses.

"Hey, Mom! Look who's here!" the pastor called to his wife as he hurried out the door to greet us. After hugs and laughter and a "look how you've grown!" to each child from our host and hostess, we all went inside.

The smell of cooking apples filled the house. Mrs. Phillips was making applesauce, and Pastor Joe was helping peel. "Go on with your work," Karyn said. "We'll all come into the kitchen and help you." Mrs. Phillips gave us each an apron, and I helped with the peeling and coring.

"You're looking good!" I told Pastor Joe. "How old are you now?"

"I'm ninety-three, Doug. I'm really getting up there."

"You amaze me," I said, shaking my head.

He stopped working on the apple in his hand and leaned against the counter. "Doug, I'm not much good anymore, you know. It takes all the strength I've got to peel and core these apples, but I want to do as much as I can, for as long as I can, for as many as I can, as often as I can." His words almost made me cry, because I knew he meant it. He truly lived to bless and serve others.

With the four of us at it, we made short work of the apples. Then we washed our hands and sat around the table.

"Doug," Pastor Joe said, looking steadily at me with watery eyes, "the Lord is calling you to the ministry. I don't just think so. I *know* so. I don't know how it's going to happen. I know it's hard with a wife and children, but if God calls you, that's *His* problem. He'll work it out."

"I hope so," I said. I thought of the wasted opportunities of my life. I was hardly prepared for the ministry, so far as formal education was concerned.

"Because I believe this so strongly, I've willed all my books to you," Pastor Joe said. "Come and let me show you the library." We got up and went into his study, the ladies following. There, neatly lined up, were shelves and shelves of books.

"Where did they all come from?" I asked.

"Oh, here and there. Don't forget, I've been in the ministry for over sixty years. You accumulate a lot of stuff in that length of time."

"Yes, and he's been a mission conference president and done lots of traveling," Mrs. Phillips added. "He buys a new book everywhere he goes."

I whistled softly. There were enough books for three life-times!

"How long can you stay? Will you be here for Sabbath?" the pastor asked.

"Yes, we'll be here Sabbath, but we're leaving Sunday morning bright and early," I replied.

"Good! Why don't you preach for us? All your friends will want to see and hear you."

"I'd be glad to, Pastor," I assured him.

After a wonderful Sabbath with friends, we returned to New Mexico to continue the work there with the Navajos. A couple of weeks later we received word that Pastor Phillips had died. He fell out of bed during the night and was too weak to get up. His wife tried to lift him back into bed, but she just couldn't do it.

"Don't worry, Mom," he said. "Just cover me up here on the floor. I'm comfortable." She covered him up, hoping to get help the next day, but by morning he was gone. I was so glad I had seen him two weeks before.

One day the telephone rang. "This is Richard Schwartz, ministerial secretary for the Northern California Conference," the voice said. I remembered meeting him a few times in passing. "Doug, we've heard of your success with the Navajos, and we're exploring the possibility of your coming to northern California to do some pastor/evangelism work. Do you think you'd be interested?"

Would I! With my home and friends in northern California, it sounded too good to be true, but I tried to not sound too excited.

"Is there any particular church that you have in mind?" I asked.

"Well, yes," he answered, "there are a couple we're considering. One is in a small town called Covelo. You may not have heard of it."

My head reeled. Out of the 130 Adventist churches in northern California, this was the church above all others I would want to pastor!

Karyn kicked me. "Say Yes!" she whispered. But even though my mind was already made up, I knew I should take it to the Lord first.

"We'll talk it over and pray about it," I said. "I'll be in touch."

Karyn said, "I'll pack while you pray."

If this wasn't a miracle, I never saw one! I needed a church like Covelo, because the people there knew I didn't know what I was doing, but they loved me anyway. Our old friends were thrilled to have me return as their pastor.

When I finally got there, I discovered how *much* I didn't know about pastoring. I didn't even know how to conduct a board meeting. I made motions and then seconded them myself! But the people bore with me patiently and loved me through it all. With God's blessing, the congregation grew and prospered. We bought the property next door and built an addition on the church.

Along with my pastoral duties, I was also expected to conduct evangelistic meetings. I held my first series of meetings right in Covelo. About 100 people attended that first night, and the attendance remained good throughout the series. At the end, 12 people took their stand for Christ and were baptized that year. The church grew during my short ministry there from 86 to 112.

Evangelism began taking more and more of my time, and I finally put in a request to be relieved of my pastoral duties so I could do evangelism full time. Recently, I made it home again to Covelo and preached on Sabbath morning. As I looked out into the congregation, I saw so many people I felt very close to. Char was one of the first people we met when we moved to Covelo. She was a hippie in those days, and so were we. I invited her to the meetings, and now here she was, a faithful church member, and so was her mother Pauline.

In response to her grandmother's pleading, the Phillipses' granddaughter Edwina had attended the meetings, and now was a faithful church member. Mrs. Phillips said over and over, "If only Joe could see that you came back to pastor the church he built, he'd be so proud of you! If only Joe could see that his granddaughter was baptized from your meetings, he'd be so happy!" And she'd cry.

Then there was John. This man had been raised in the church, but left as a young man and attended a Presbyterian church during most of the thirty years he had been out. When the evangelistic meetings began, he came faithfully and was the first person I ever baptized. Now he was a strong member, taught a Sabbath School class, and had married Char's mother.

And Marta! Seeing Marta brought back some of my favorite memories. It's a long story, but I think it's worth the telling. Even though I had mixed feelings about Easter sunrise services, I decided to attend. It was good to fellowship with the other ministers in town, and I never tired of the story of the Resurrection. They asked me to have the morning prayer, so I put on my suit and tie and went downtown.

After the service, I climbed into my car and headed for home, but as I passed the Pentecostal Faith Tabernacle, I felt a strong urge to stop and go in. I felt that I was supposed to preach there that day. "But why should I do that?" I asked myself. "I'm the pastor of the Adventist church."

I drove on by, but I had a strong feeling that I was disobeying God, so I turned around and started back. "How do I know this isn't just my own wild imagination?" I continued arguing with myself. "Am I supposed to walk into the church and march up the aisle and tell the pastor, 'The Lord told me I'm supposed to preach here this morning, so you can go and sit down'? I must be tired!" Again I passed by.

I don't remember how many times I drove by, arguing with myself and praying for guidance. Finally I drove home to eat breakfast. I ripped off my tie and laid it on the dresser. I went to the refrigerator and got out a banana, but the impression returned, and I felt I was running away, like Jonah. "Well, Lord, I don't understand this, but I guess I'd better go." So I put my tie back on and started out the door.

"Where are you going?" Karyn asked.

"To church," I said.

"Oh?" That was all she said. She wasn't surprised, because I often acted strangely. I drove back and parked in front of the Faith tabernacle. As I walked in I saw that the service was in progress, and the minister had just invited the congregation to kneel and pray for the outpouring of the Spirit before the preaching. I slipped into a back pew and knelt down.

Prayer in a Pentecostal service isn't like that of most churches. They pray a long time, and they don't just pray quietly in their hearts. Some pray out loud, some mumble, and some speak in tongues. The lady beside me sounded as though she was talking about Japanese motorcycles. As for me, I asked the Lord to let me know if He brought me here, or if this was just my own imagining.

While I was praying, I got this mental picture that when they finished praying, the pastor was going to ask me to come up and preach. "But what would I say?" I thought as I knelt there praying. Then a whole sermon came to me, just as if it were being handed out, about Mary Magdalene representing the church.

The praying reached a kind of crescendo and then began to quiet down as one and then another of the people took their seats. I rose from my knees and sat back in the pew. Then Pastor Ray Hull stepped up to the podium and looked directly at me and said, "I see that our Adventist brother is here today. Pastor, do you have a few words to say for the Lord this morning?"

I knew he meant, "Do you have a testimony?" My heart raced, but I tried to conceal my excitement. As calmly as I could, I stood up. "You know how it is, Pastor," I said. "We preachers can't just say a *few* words." I smiled and started to sit down, but before I could, he came right back.

"Then why don't you come on up and preach?" My heart started skipping in my chest, and I thought, "This can't be really happening." As I walked toward the front with my Bible in hand,

118

I had never felt more confident that I was just where God wanted me, because He had brought me to this church in such a remarkable manner. I knew He would instruct me and give me words to say.

I fairly walked on air as I made my way up to the pulpit and opened my Bible to John 8. Everything seemed like it was rehearsed. I began to talk about the woman taken in adultery, and the words just flowed from my mouth, almost without effort on my part. I heard an abundance of Amens, Praise the Lords, and Preach it, brother! That told me the audience was with me, and it warmed my heart. (I wish they would do more of that in Adventist churches.)

At the end I made an altar call. Many people came forward, and we had prayer together. As the last of the people were leaving, Pastor Hull turned to me with tears streaming down his cheeks. "Pastor Doug," he said with choked voice, "God sent you here this morning."

I wondered how he knew.

"I've been sick," he went on. "I didn't know what I was going to do, so I've been praying about it. I asked my wife to preach, but she was scared to death. So you see, Brother Doug, God sent you in answer to my prayer."

Since that day, I have never doubted that God has His people in every church, regardless of their creed or doctrine. He hears and answers their prayers, too, and before Jesus comes, we'll all be united into one body that keeps the commandments of God and faith of Jesus (see Revelation 14:12). Before I left that day, he invited me to come again, and I promised him I would.

Now, that's how I met Marta. I did come back to visit that Faith tabernacle another Sunday, and when I did, I noticed a Spanish lady seated in front of me. I could tell that she didn't speak English, so I sent up a quick prayer that the Lord would help me make friends with her. Right after I prayed, the pastor said, "Now stand up and shake hands with the people around you." I could see that God had opened the way, so while people were greeting each other, I said, *"¿Como está usted, hermana?"* ("How are you, sister?") I had learned a little Spanish from a Mexican friend who lived with me.

She broke into a big smile when she heard her own language. She began to rattle off Spanish faster than I could understand. I held up my hand. *"Despacio,"* I said. *"¡Mas lento!"* ("Speak slowly.") Then, using my halting Spanish, I asked, "Do you understand what's being said here?"

"No," she said, "but this is God's house, so I come."

"I go to church on Saturday, and we have several members who speak Spanish. Come and visit us next Saturday," I invited.

"Gracias, señor," she said, and sure enough she was in my church the next Sabbath. Before long she had her children coming too. Now, both she and the children are faithful members of our church, and all the children attend our little church school. So as I looked out into the Adventist congregation that Sabbath, I rejoiced to see Marta and her children.

Not long after that, as we were on our way to prayer meeting one evening, we saw an ambulance in front of Mrs. Phillips's home. She had suffered a stroke, and a couple of days later she died without regaining consciousness. Her granddaughter found her Bible lying on the table beside her chair with the lesson booklet. It was Wednesday, and she had filled in the Wednesday section of answers in her own shaky handwriting. Her last written words that morning were, "We will not die."

Everyone dies the first death, of course, but the righteous will not die the second death mentioned in Revelation 20. Of that, Mrs. Phillips had absolute confidence.

It was my privilege to conduct her funeral service. The church overflowed with her friends and neighbors, and flowers were everywhere. It seemed almost like a celebration. A great warrior had won the victory over sin and laid down her armor. There she lay at peace, beyond the reach of Satan. I couldn't feel sorry for her. In fact, I envied her. The next thing she will hear will be the voice of Jesus calling her forth from the grave as promised in 1 Thessalonians 4:16, 17. She'll feel the surge of eternal life coursing through her immortal body, and she'll be with her beloved Joe. What a reunion that will be! Together they will walk the streets of gold in that glorious city described in the last two chapters in the Bible.

After the funeral I went to visit her son. He still had not given his heart to the Lord, and I hoped I might find some encouraging words to speak to him.

"You know that your mother loved you very much, and she prayed for you every day," I said. "She kept praying for you to the very last."

"Yes, I know," he said, "but don't hold your breath praying for me."

What could I say to this hard-drinking, rough-talking, macho man that would reach his heart? "If you'd known me a few years ago, you'd never have believed that I would ever be a Christian either. Your parents had a lot to do with my being where I am today. They were real saints."

"I know. They were saints," he said quietly. He looked down and fiddled with his hat. "But they were not always that way. They *became* saints."

Now those words gave *me* hope. I could become a saint. When I look at Jesus' perfect example, I say, "I may have a long way to go," but when I look back and see how far He has brought me, it gives me courage. I know He's not done with me yet. If I let Him, He'll finish what He's started in my life, and some day take me home.

18

The Rock That Would Not Roll

Not long ago I brought my family to southern California for a brief vacation. We found a nice little hotel in Desert Hot Springs with a beautiful view of the mountain that was once my home.

"Dad, let's hike to your cave." Micah, my second child and oldest boy, was always fascinated with cave stories. Rachel preferred shopping with her mom, and Daniel, age five, was much too young for such a grueling trip.

Early the next morning Karyn dropped Micah and me off in Palm Springs with our backpacks. As we walked through town, I noticed how much things had changed. The old Mayfair Market was closed and boarded up. My street friends were gone. The Faith Center Church that we used to attend had moved. Even as we started up the canyon, things looked different.

It had been eight years since I hiked this trail. In that time there had been a fire on Mt. San Jacinto, as well as a moderate earthquake and a major flood in the area. Trees that were once landmarks along the path were now only blackened stumps. In many spots the old trail had washed out and been relocated. Even the creek had changed its course.

Though Micah was only seven, he plugged along like a real soldier, never complaining about the heat or the small backpack he carried.

Part way up the mountain I pointed ahead. "We'll stop up there at Square Pool," I said. "It's a great place to stop and dive in, swim around, and cool off." But when we got to Square Pool, we found that it had been filled in with sand. We could only walk across it and take a shower in the waterfall nearby.

I began to wonder if my cave would still be there. What would I find?

After about two-and-a-half hours of hiking uphill, we reached the highest point of the trip—the spot about 4,000 feet above Palm Springs with a panoramic view of all the desert cities. We sat for about ten minutes, drinking in the spectacular scene. We also drank some water.

After our brief rest, we shouldered our packs and started the trip down into the third valley. Things were beginning to look more familiar, and my heart began beating faster—more from excitement than from hiking. As we rounded the ridge and beheld the third valley directly before us, I stopped a moment to breathe and take in the scene.

"Watcha lookin' at, Dad?" Micah asked.

"My rock," I replied softly.

At that point we were surrounded by rocks, and my statement might have sounded strange to a person who could not see what we saw. But one rock in that valley stood out like a basketball in a box of marbles. I had lived in the shadow of that giant boulder for a year and a half. Hundreds of times, after climbing 4,000 feet up desolate desert mountains in one of the hottest climates on earth, I had rounded this ridge and beheld "my rock." For me it represented rest and shade. It meant that home was in sight, with food and water. Sometimes there were earthquakes in these mountains, and rocks and dirt would come tumbling down the valley walls from all directions, but I was never afraid under the protection of "my rock."

After all those years, seeing it again, unchanged, brought tears to my eyes. "Come on, Micah," I said. "We're almost there now." I wanted to keep moving before he noticed the water sprouting in my eyes.

In about ten minutes we were on the valley floor, hiking along Tahquitz Creek. I could not help reminiscing. "Over there is where I had my sauna, Micah." I pointed off to one side of the trail. "I would heat up big rocks in a fire, then carry them with a shovel into a plastic tepee, seal the door with me inside, and pour on hot water. In a few minutes I would be so hot that I would have to rush out and dive into that large pool over there."

Micah listened, wide-eyed with fascination.

In a few moments we climbed between two rocks and over a log that opened into my "cave yard." Very little had changed. The smoke-blackened ceiling, my rock-log chair and fireplace, were all still the same. Some of the sand in the bedroom cave and main floor had washed away, but it still felt like home.

Micah could not contain his excitement. Even though I am sure he was tired, he dropped his pack and went off exploring. I rested a few minutes before unpacking and pitching camp. When Micah returned, we took a swim in the pool. This time of year the water felt refreshingly cool.

We sat in the fading sunlight to dry off. "Micah, it will soon be dark," I said. "We'd better fetch some wood for the fire tonight." By sundown we had a huge pile of wood and furious appetites, so we built a fire and cooked up some of our provisions.

"Dad," Micah said as he finished his last spoonful of beans, "where did you find that Bible that was in the cave?"

I pointed toward the cave. "See that rock ledge by my bedroom cave? That's where it was."

"Whatever happened to it?"

"Not long after I started reading it I accidentally dropped it in the creek," I said. "After that it swelled up, and it wasn't very easy to read, so my friend Glen gave me a new one. I'm not sure what ever became of the first one."

We had our evening prayer and threw some more sticks on the fire. But long after Micah had crawled into his sleeping bag, he kept asking questions about life in this wild canyon.

Finally he was silent, and I knew that he had dropped off to sleep. The light from the fire danced on the cave walls, creating familiar images. Then a little kangaroo rat hopped across the cave floor, stopped a moment and looked at me as if to ask, "Where have you been?" and then hopped away. I reached into my backpack and felt around for the Bible I had brought along. I opened it at random, and in the light from the fire I read Matthew 7:24, 25. Jesus was speaking. "Whosoever heareth these sayings of mine, and doeth them, I will liken him unto a wise man, which built his house upon a rock: and the rain descended, and the floods came, and the winds blew, and beat upon that house; and it fell not: for it was founded upon a rock."

I thought, "How many times in the Bible Jesus is compared to a rock. He is called the chief Cornerstone, the sure Foundation, and the Stone cut from the mountain. Even the Ten Commandments were written on stone to represent how unchanging they are. One of my favorite symbols of Christ, from Isaiah 32:2, compares Jesus to a mighty rock that gives shade in a weary land. Just as my cave boulder has stood through rain, wind, fire, and earthquake, unchanging and unmoved, so Jesus has always been there for me, dependable, loving, providing shelter from spiritual heat and cold."

With these happy thoughts I set the Bible on the ledge and crawled into my bag. I don't know whether the ground was harder or I had become softer, but it took me a while to get comfortable. But soon I drifted off to sleep with the sound of the creek talking to me.

Micah had a hard time waking up the next morning. His eyes were half-opened, and it was comical, watching him look around, trying to remember where he was and how he got there. His hair looked like he had combed it all night with an eggbeater!

"We'll need to get an early start down the hill to meet Mom in town," I said as I opened a can for breakfast.

"But, Dad, we just got here."

"I know, Son, but our vacation time is about over. Let's be glad we had a chance to visit this place."

"OK," Micah said with a sigh.

After eating our breakfast, taking a quick bath in the pool, and saying a short prayer, we packed up our things and took one last look around. As I started out of the cave yard, Micah called to me. "Dad, you left your Bible on the ledge over there!"

"I know, Son."

He seemed to understand, and we started our trip down the mountain.

"Dad?" Micah spoke after a long silence.

"Yes, Son."

"Do you ever miss living up here?"

I didn't have to think long to answer. "Yes, Son, I do. In many ways life was much simpler up here. There were no pressures, no stresses."

"Dad."

I could tell that the wheels in his mind were turning.

"Do you think you will ever move back up here?"

"No, Son, God didn't call us to run away from the world. Jesus said we should go into all the world and preach the gospel."

We both grew silent as we continued down the trail. I was thinking my thoughts, and in his own childish way, I knew that Micah was thinking his. I was so thankful for all my children, and I felt particularly close to Micah this morning as we hiked along together. God has shown me many things about His love through my children, and Micah taught me one of the greatest lessons I've ever learned.

One morning about five years earlier, when we were living in Covelo, Karyn and I found him in his crib moaning and staring blankly at the ceiling. We knew something was seriously wrong, so Karyn scooped him up in her arms and we raced to the nearest hospital, forty miles away. We rushed into the emergency room with our blue-eyed bundle, and after a basic examination, the young intern who was on call that morning told us he feared that Micah had spinal meningitis. He said that the only way to be sure was to do a test called a "spinal tap." That involved inserting a three-inch needle between the vertebrae in Micah's spine. The spine, of course, is filled with nerves.

Micah was at the age when he could talk a little. He said things like "Mommy," "Daddy," and "banana." I wondered what was going through his mind right then. Karyn left the room, saying she couldn't bear to watch. I stood by as a couple of nurses held my baby boy on his side, bent so his back was arched. This evidently caused Micah a great deal of pain, because Micah started groaning. The saddest part was that the intern confessed having little experience in doing spinal taps. So I watched with a breaking heart as three or four times the young doctor pushed the needle into my little boy's back. Only a parent can understand the heartache of watching a child suffer.

Micah looked up and cried out over and over, "Daddy, Daddy, Daddy."

This tore me apart. I knew he wondered, "Why are you letting these people hurt me? Don't you love me anymore?" And I knew that at his age, there was no way I could make him understand. One of my greatest fears was that Micah might die thinking that I didn't love him.

As it turned out, he did have spinal meningitis, but by the grace of God and ten days in the hospital he completely recovered. But after that I could never read the story of Jesus on the cross, crying out to His Father, "My God, my God, why have You forsaken me?" without thinking of this experience. It would have been much easier for me to suffer than to watch one of my children suffer, and I know that our Father in heaven loved His Son, Jesus, much more than I love my children.

How could He do it?

The only conclusion I can reach is that God and Christ loved us so desperately that they were willing to go through with this terrible ordeal in spite of the pain.

This is why I told Micah that God has called me to preach the gospel. I feel driven to tell the world about a God who loves us that much. It is my prayer that those who read the testimony in this book will learn from my experience that happiness does not come from the abundance of things. I learned the hard way that the happiness the world offers is not real. It's the Big Lie. But the joy of serving God and ministering to my fellow man is genuine, and it leaves no hangover.

I know, because I tried it all!

Other Books
by Doug Batchelor

To See the King
Seven Steps to Salvation

By comparing his own true life experiences with those described in Isaiah 6:1-8, Doug Batchelor shows that understanding and experiencing salvation is not at all difficult.

How to Survive and Thrive in Church

This lively volume provides an excellent resource for just about anyone who has struggles in their relationship with the church. Regardless of your church experience, you will find each chapter oozes with practical principles helpful for surviving and thriving in a big, small, dead, divided, scandal-torn or gossip-ridden church. This book is dedicated to exposing some (not all) of the devil's most common traps and tricks used to catapult people out of church fellowship.

At Jesus' Feet:
The Gospel According to Mary Magdalene

Doug Batchelor unveils the beauty of the gospel through the eyes of Jesus' most dedicated disciple. Discover a fresh picture of a gentle, loving Saviour who, without condemning or condoning our past, offers us a new future as we, like Mary, linger at Jesus' feet. The book is divided into two parts—the story and the study. Most of the study sections also contain some good stories!

Broken Chains:
Finding Peace for the Raging Soul

Have you ever reached the brink of despair, feeling that your personality flaws, bad habits and selfishness have placed you beyond the reach of redemption? Then this book is for you . . . and it is for me.

These books may be purchased from your local Book Center or from

Mountain Ministry
5431 Auburn Blvd., Suite A-1
Sacramento, CA 95841
or by phone at 916-332-5800

School Days

My family and ministry have experienced tremendous transitions since the completion of *The Richest Caveman* book in 1988. God continues to preserve, lead and bless. These pictures represent both times of joy and times of challenge in my life. I am simply one of countless testimonies of the mercy of God's grace. He has been so good to me! It is my prayer that you, too, will be able to look back in your life and see God's hand leading.

Doug Batchelor

New York Military Academy was the elementary step to West Point. We had several different dress uniforms that were impressive. This is my first year at NYMA.

My friend, Bobby Boyer is on the left and that's me on the right.

The second year I had the rank of sergeant and a row of medals. I was only 11 years of age. See Page 10 of this book.

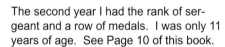
ITALY

This is my first passport picture taken before leaving for Genoa, Italy, to enroll in the ocean-going Flint School Abroad. I had taken LSD the day before and my eyes were still dilated. Story on page 42.

Right: You can see Palm Springs as you look back over the dangerous cougar trail on the way up to my cave high in the San Jacinto Mountains. Many hikers have been killed or injured on this treacherous pathway. See page 52.

Left: This picture was taken in 1974 during the only visit by my brother, Falcon. We are on our way up to the cave after getting supplies in Palm Springs. This exhausting climb represented a tremendous accomplishment for Falcon because of his cystic fibrosis.

Right: I enjoyed taking my family up to my cave in 1995. It's a grueling three-hour trek over boulders, cactus and loose rocks. I was impressed by how well they managed the difficult climb! This trip marked 22 years from my first hike up the mountain at age 15 with Jim and Sunny. See page 31.

Cave Life

Left: Here's my cave. I'm sitting on my rock and log throne, holding my cat, Stranger. See page 65. This is where I spent hundreds of hours looking up the trail while I cooked, ate and read my Bible. I had everything placed around my chair so it could easily be reached See Page 54.

Right: In the years that have passed since I lived in this cave, the surrounding area has experienced floods, fires and earthquakes. But I found my cave has not changed much. On one of my return visits, I left another Bible in plain view for the next "traveler." See page 125.

Left: When my son, Micah, was only 7 years of age, I went back to my cave for the first time in years. You can see Micah swimming in the refreshing pool just outside of the cave. In the summer months this pool would stop flowing and I had to hike up the canyon for clean drinking water. See page 124.

Left: My mother flew up to the cave in a helicopter with the NBC news team and camera crew. Reporter Bill Applegate did an excellent human interest interview as to why the son of a millionaire was living in a cave. The program aired nationally three times that day. I had just become a Christian and had prayed for an opportunity to witness. I was stunned by how quickly and abundantly God answered my prayer! See page 77.

Right: This is my first business, Batchelor's Wholesale Prime Beef Steaks and my VW Bug. Because of what I learned about meat, I have been a vegetarian ever since. See page 93.

Pastor Joe and Miriam Phillips were the finest examples of living Christianity I have ever met. Consistently kind and self-sacrificing, their greatest joy was to introduce others to Jesus. I will always be eternally grateful for their love to me. See pages 95 & 111. This is the Covelo Church in 1996. I was baptized here by Pastor Joe Phillips, and then on two different occasions I returned to pastor this wonderful congregation. See page 116.

My Family

Right: Mom and Dad during happy times. Opposites do attract, at least temporarily. For example, she was a Democrat and he was a Republican.

Left: This was a rare moment for the four of us together. It was the occasion of Falcon and Sandy's wedding. He was 25 and I was 23. Can you spot the "black sheep" of the family?

This is the last picture taken of the three of us—Falcon, Dad and me. Falcon suffered with cystic fibrosis. He fought the disease courageously and survived until he was 35. I was by his side when he died in July 1990, just a week after this picture was taken.

Here I am with Mom and Falcon at summer camp. When we were older, Falcon started a camp in the Florida Keys for children with C.F. I helped several years as a camp counselor and pastor.

Mom With The Stars

Clint Eastwood

Sally Field

George Burns

Mohammed Ali

The Three Stooges
(Curley, Mo & Larry)

Dustin Hoffman

Paul Newman

Natalie Wood

My mother, Ruth, was involved in one aspect or another of show business all her life. She wrote songs for Elvis Presley, musical plays, and did a number of small parts in big movies and TV specials. She could play the guitar, sing, paint, and do almost anything artistic without formal training. She found her niche when she began working as a film critic in 1975 until her untimely death from cancer in July 1992. See page 5.

My Dad

World War II found my father, George, flying for the U.S. Air Force in Europe. He had a keen mind and sharp business sense. He began building his empire after his discharge through buying, selling, and leasing aircraft.

Because he has given generously to a wide variety of charities, my Father was chosen as "Outstanding Citizen" and has been featured in several newspapers, business magazines and aviation journals.

Dad was always a dynamo of activity. In addition to running several companies, he raced cars, flew jets, water skied, and sailed his own yacht. He suffered a stroke in 1994 that forced him to slow his pace. See page 8. After a short illness, Dad passed away in July 2002 from cancer.

Left: This is our family on a visit to my grandparents, Al and Lil Tarshis, my mother's parents. Their name comes from the Biblical town to which the Prophet Jonah ran. I lived with Grandma and "Poppy" several times after Mom and Dad divorced. They planted the first seeds in my young mind that there was a God watching over me.

(Left to right) Daniel, Karen and Stephen, Poppy, Doug, Grandma, Micah and Rachael.

Right: This picture was taken in June 1999. Included are all our children. From left to right is Daniel, Stephen, Rachael, Doug, Micah, Nathan, Karen, and Cheri. Cheri is my daughter from a teenage romance during my cave days. (Not everything is in the book!) In April 2001 Micah suffered a fatal accident when the tractor he was unloading rolled over.

Left: Currently I am serving as Senior Pastor of the Sacramento Central Church and President-Speaker for Amazing Facts Ministries, a radio, TV, evangelistic ministry. I continue to travel with my family preaching the Gospel all over the world. Here we are in Sydney, Australia where I spoke in the area ten times in ten days! It's not all vacation! We are thankful for God's protection and care!